D1460554

WHEN STEAM WAS KING AT BRIGHTON

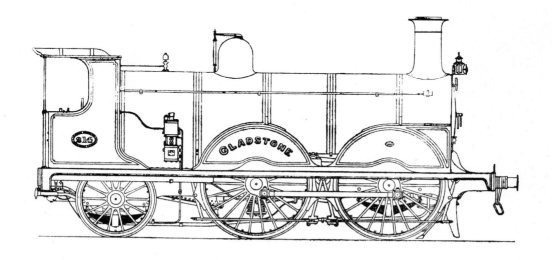

"H1" Atlantics Nos 39 and 38 under repair in Erecting Shop.

The electricians shop. Generators and batteries for carriage lighting in foreground.

When Steam was King at Brighton

The general offices as seen from Central Station. The high roof of the "Iron Man" riveter building in left background. Driver Harry Funnell relaxes in the cab before leaving for Victoria. c. 1925.

A nostalgic glimpse into the old Brighton works, the machines and the men of the Age of Steam.

A. C. PERRYMAN

incorporating the earlier book *Life at Brighton Loco. Works*

ROCHESTER PRESS

By the same author:
Life at the Brighton Loco Works (Oakwood Press), The Brighton Baltics (Oakwood Press), Steam on the Brighton Line (Bradford Barton), A Clubman at Brooklands (Haynes);
and for Rochester Press: Bygone LBSCR Steam volumes 1 and 2.

A.C. Perryman was apprenticed at the Brighton Loco Works in early Southern Region days, when it ran very much as it had done as the L.B.&S.C. Railway. He came into contact with every part of a steam locomotive's anatomy the hard, old fashioned way, by practical experience! When the Southern Railway decided to run down the Brighton Works, the staff were laid off and the young ex-apprentices advised to seek other employment. The author then left and entered the motor trade, until war in 1939 claimed him for munition work. After the war and sensing the demise of steam power on the railways, he decided on a 'locomotive works' of his own and created some outstanding models of his old Brighton favourites (depicted in this book), from official works drawings. These are now the only three-dimensional reminders of the large Brighton express locos which graced the Sussex landscape. He has recently completed two small volumes of photographic reminiscences of the L.B.&S.C. Railway for the Rochester Press.

First published as Life at the Brighton Loco Works by Oakwood Press, this revised and enlarged edition © A.C. Perryman 1982

ISBN 0 946379 009

Designed by Malcolm John for the Rochester Press, 38 High Street, Chatham, Kent.

Set in 12 point Plantin, 2 point leaded by M.C. Typeset, Rochester, Kent
Printed by Mackays of Chatham Ltd, Lordswood, Chatham, Kent

Contents

The L.B.&S.C.R.'s Brighton Terminus in Queens Road, Brighton, September 28-9-1913. Note the fashions of the period!

Inside Brighton's Central Station with trains at platforms 1 and 2, the West Coast Line.

Foreword

This is a book which should be read by everybody interested in Steam-operated Railways and Locomotives, written from first-hand experience. Such experience is no longer available, and those possessing it are a rapidly diminishing band. It deals with an aspect of Railway operation which has been very much neglected; admittedly it is a far less glamoroous side than locomotive driving, but it is at least equally important, for without the Building and Repairing Departments, steam railways would very rapidly have come to a complete stand-still. Of course, previous to nationalization, all the Railways had locomotives built by outside firms (not excluding foreign ones, German and American), but the maintenance and repair was entirely carried out by the Railways themselves and this book gives an excellent picture of all the differing phases of work in a Locomotive plant, and has the great advantage of having been compiled from first-hand experience, obviously aided by an excellent memory. I served an apprenticeship with a big Midland firm of general engineers from 1903–08 and stayed on there for another four years. There was no sort of formal training for apprentices in those days, and from Mr. Perryman's account it is obvious that this was still the case in his days. His story brought back to me many nostalgic memories, particularly about the tricks and practical jokes, and also about the wide variety of human characters which closely parallel my own earlier experience.

In my day, hours were much longer, a fifty-four hour week, often with a lot of overtime and week-end work, and Technical School on top of such long hours, was, in my opinion, largely farcical; after a nine-and-a-half hour day, one was hardly in a condition to absorb instruction, or take any real interest in it, but it was part of the routine. Pay too was very low; I started at the magnificent rate of four shillings a week.

Today, the apprentice with a good Company has a very different life. He probably spends a couple of years in a well equipped apprentice training department, staffed by highly competent instructors, qualified in both theory and practice, is given time off, paid, to attend special classes at Technical School or Polytechnic, and if he is of the right type, has an excellent chance of going to a University and obtaining an Engineering Degree. This is all to the good, but I think the apprentice *does* miss something by things being made so comparatively easy for him. I think he misses the stimulus of being on his own, and dependent upon his own initiative and guts. In these days of specialization, the modern apprentice does not get the very wide range of experience that his fore-runner did in the earlier years of the century, which range is well brought out in this book. Today, specialization is a very real necessity for most engineers, but for the man who is likely to find himself working out in the wilds, far from civilization and entirely dependent on his own resources, the old type of training is still invaluable.

I have enjoyed this book and it draws a most accurate picture of conditions in what now we must regard as a past age. Mr. Perryman has done his work well.

Rustington, 1971

K. N. Harris

VICTORIA STATION. (L B & S C R)

The Northern end of the Railway. Victoria Station in the early 1900's. Grosvenor Hotel in the
Background.

The entrance to the works from the platforms of Central Station is obscured by "E1" class 0-6-0 tank
No. 607, still retaining its copper topped chimney in the early 1920's. The iron foundry's chimney is
visible near the signal post.

Preface

This book deals with the closing years of the "Golden Age" of railways, which reached its heyday about 1910. From then on, it began to decline; very slowly at first, but hastened by the Great War of 1914–18; it never recovered, because of the increase in motor traffic after the war.

The Grouping of 1923 formed the many independent companies into four groups, and the old L.B.S.C.R. was merged into the "Southern Railway". The Works at Brighton carried on in early Southern days just as they had in "Brighton" days. Changes came about later, but they were very gradual.

During my stay at the Works, from October 1928 until March 1936, I saw the Works staff dwindle from about 2,000 to about 150 men, under the Southern's "running down" policy for Brighton Works.

Most of the machinery was removed to Ashford or Eastleigh, and the rest broken up, and I had the somewhat melancholy job of performing this latter task. The men also, were transferred to the other Works above. Others left, some were sacked; few remained.

Even the apprentices were given a week's notice upon completing their training. It was then stepped up: their notice was given a week early, so they left on the day they finished their time!

With two to go before it was my turn, the rot stopped! We were offered temporary jobs as fitters, to enable us to find other jobs. I was one of the few that did find another job in those years of depression, and so left. What was left of the others hung on, and in three years more the Second World War burst upon us.

My old chargehand's words came true. When I was in the millwrights gang, breaking up the old machinery, he nearly wept, and said, "Ah! it wants another war, and we would be putting brand new machinery in here as fast as we could!" And so it came to pass, although I was not there to see it. Men were taken on wholesale. A lot returned. I had the chance to go back; was even asked to go. But it was too late! I had now got settled elsewhere and deemed it prudent not to turn the clock back.

New locomotives were turned out by the score, but the end of Steam was in sight, and the Works finally closed for locomotive purposes in March 1958. After ten years of fulfilling various roles, mainly to do with its old competitor, the motor car, British Rail decided to demolish it.

The first loco to be built had left on May 17th, 1852, so the Works lasted for locomotive purposes for almost 106 years.

This book is dedicated to that ever-dwindling band of stalwarts who helped me acquire my engineering training, the men "behind the scenes" who made and serviced my beloved steam locomotives. Almost without exception they loved their work, which was often dirty, uncomfortable, and sometimes dangerous. When I had finished my training and was employed as a fitter (1st Class) my wage was the princely sum of £2 5s. per week for 48½ hours. Many men were bringing up a family on this, although I don't know how!

Most of the illustrations depict the Works in L.B.S.C.R. days before I was there, but they had changed but little during my time. Few of these rare shots have ever been published before. I am indebted to Mr. M. Joly for his assistance in supplying these nostalgic scenes from his private collection, and correcting the script.

On then, to describe some of the happiest working days of my life, though certainly the least rewarding financially.

Sompting, Sussex, 1970   A. C. Perryman

Reference No.

$(\frac{7}{28})$ **SOUTHERN RAILWAY.** $(\frac{Stock.}{1791.})$

CHIEF MECHANICAL ENGINEER'S DEPARTMENT,

BRIGHTON.   WORKS,   25th October, 19 33

THIS IS TO CERTIFY that   ALBERT CHARLES PERRYMAN

has completed an apprenticeship of   five years   ---   months at these

Works as   Fitter --

and that his conduct during that period has been   satisfactory.

Further particulars respecting his capabilities will be

supplied on application by prospective employers.

[signature]

Chief Mechanical Engineer.

Chapter One

Growing Up to Steam

It all began early in World War I. I was nearly two years old when the balloon went up in Serbia. My father was on one of his periodic visits to his ageing mother in Essex, and I was taken along as well. Upon arrival at Liverpool Street there was some time before the train went, so a fond mother had stood me down on the platform, and whilst talking to Dad, had not noticed that I was using my new found powers of locomotion.

By the time they had missed me, I was nowhere to be seen. There was, however, a small crowd of people gathered near one of the locomotives belonging to the old Great Eastern Railway, and to this they made their way.

Now Liverpool Street was never renowed as one of the cleanest stations in London; with complete disregard for this, I had decided to lie full length on the platform in my "Sunday best", to try and look underneath the loco. A kindly driver had left his cab and come up to see that I came to no harm, or that I did not get mixed up in his beloved loco's motion, I expect! Anyway I was returned to my anxious parents' control, none the worse for my adventure; except that my "Sunday best" hardly looked its best from then on! The driver's parting words were, "Ah! we shall soon be having him along with us!"

It was obvious from then on that I was born with the "bug" in me, an inborn love for the steam locomotive, man's most exciting creation.

As the war progressed, and Zeppelins started to raid London, it was deemed prudent to evacuate my elder sister and myself to my aunt in Somerset. I don't remember much of the journey down, but I do vividly remember being rudely awakened from a nice snooze, and dumped down on a cold platform, on a dark, very wet night. By the time the train had departed, I was crying, louder and louder. Nothing seemed to pacify me, until, coming out of the darkness nearly at right angles to us, were two light engines coupled together. As they passed under one of the station lamps I could see they were both blue. The crying stopped as if by magic. The engines were parted. One went back into the yard beyond, and the other reappeared a little later with a couple of suburban coaches. We boarded these and were transported to Burnham-on-Sea.

11

Some time was spent there with my aunt, and all my life I could vaguely remember a blue tank engine in a little shed of its own, right down on the beach. I could never think where it was, until quite recently, I had a holiday at Weston-super-Mare, and was exploring "Somerset and Dorset" terrain. We went to Burnham-on-Sea, parked the car and walked along the front, and when we came to the remains of the old station, there it was, plain to see, even after all those years. You could still see the decrepit level crossing gates, and where the rails had once crossed the road to that tiny little shed on the beach.

I retraced my journey of all those years ago, and came to – Highbridge. The overbridge was still there, and so was the old S. & D. Works, now alas, derelict. I could at once see how those two locos could come out of the darkness, almost at right angles and envelop me in their steam, on that miserable wet night fifty years ago. Until that chance meeting with Highbridge, the H.Q. of the S. & D., and junction with the G.W. main line, I used to think that my memory of that night was just a dream.

When it was deemed safe for us to return, we came back to London and my next memories are of the railings, flanking the L.B. & S.C.R. main line past Clapham Common. My father often took me to the common on his "leave" days from the police force, and I used to spend all my time watching the trains go by, as he sat on the seat smoking his pipe!

After the war, he retired from the police, left London, and we went to live in Queens Road, Haywards Heath, only about ¼ mile from the station. This was absolutely ideal for me, and I spent a good deal of time on Haywards Heath "down" platform, watching the evening commuter trains thunder through! This was the era of the slip coaches on the Brighton, and after the "fast" had torn through, whistle shrieking, I would watch the slip come gently to a stand. A tank engine would then come out of the bay and back on to the slip, to take it through "All stations to Brighton".

What days they were for train spotters! Several of us schoolboys would gather and watch the line for hours at a time, notebooks in hand. Not only numbers did we collect. Many of the Brighton express engines had names too! Not quite so exotic as the L.N.W.R. "Thunderer" and "Audacious" etc., or the Great Western "Shooting Star" and "Great Bear", but we often used to see one or another of "Arthur Otway", "Samuel Laing", "Cottesloe", "Stroudley", "Gladstone", "J. Gay", "Bessemer", the two-domed "Leconfield", "Devonshire", "Princess Royal", "Prince of Wales", "His Majesty", "Norfolk", "Billinton", "La France" (one of my special favourites). "Abergavenny", "Bessborough" and the mightly "Charles C. Macrae" and "Stephenson".

"Bessborough" quite frequently went through with the up "City Limited", and we used to wait near the station on our way to school, to see it go tearing through. The noise it made was terrific and the exhaust used to go straight up out

12

off the chimney for about six feet, before it started to curve over the cab roof, in spite of the speed being up in the seventies! The engine used to glisten and the sun always seemed to be shining, reflecting off the rods of the valve gear which always impressed us boys.

Then one or two of us had seen the lordly "Stephenson", latest express loco of the Brighton, and bigger and noisier even than "Bessborough". I knew one or two of the porters on the station, and in between their shouting "Stand back there," as some express came tearing down on us round the bend from Copyhold Junction, one had told me how the lordly "Stephenson", after hauling the "Southern Belle", had over-run the turntable at Brighton, and pushed the wall into New England Road! The wall apparently was incapable of resisting 98½ tons of Baltic tank engine, and I was to learn later that this was not the only occasion the wall had been shifted.

None of the boys of those days ever thought of vandalism. They were far too fond of the engines to think of that. I was allowed on the station without question, their only interest in me being my safety, and to stand well back as the "fasts" as they were known on the Brighton, went through!

I didn't need much telling about that either! The noise and vibration as those Atlantics and Baltics tore through, sometimes doing well over 80, when you were only a few feet away, was awe-inspiring to a schoolboy. The whistle was usually shrieking as well. When they had gone a cloud of dust would be following the last coach, with all sorts of bits of paper blowing about in its wake.

Then in 1922 we began to see what was to be the Brighton's last engine, "Remembrance", first in red oxide, and later in "shop grey", lined in black and white. It became a favourite of mine, right from the start. It was also to cause me quite a bit of pain later on, while at school at Shoreham.

The station was certainly a wonderful place for me, for besides the thrill of the "fasts" coming through, particularly in the evenings, there were a few semi-fasts which stopped at the station. I would try and be on the "up" platform for these, about opposite where the loco would stop. I then had an uninterrupted view of the rods moving when the loco started up, and could count the heavy exhaust beats as the train got under way.

In March, 1923, my family moved to Shoreham-by-Sea. I found this new location very different from the last. The house was about 100 yards from the branch line from Shoreham to Horsham, very near the level crossing for the old tollbridge. I would go and sit on the fence here, but the service was nowhere near so frequent as the main line I had left. One good feature was that the smaller classes, after overhaul at the works, used to use this line for their trial trips. Some had green wheels, and the rest of them the old Brighton "umber". Others were resplendent in a complete new coat of "sage" green, which the Southern used in the early days of grouping.

13

Now the school I went to was a good half mile nearer to the station and was almost opposite the junction of the Shoreham–Portsmouth main line and the Shoreham–Horsham branch. My classroom, even when we were sitting at our desks, gave a fine view of the railway, and I used to look up every time a train went by. A fast went by about 9.50 a.m. to Portsmouth, nearly always worked by B2X's; either 171 or 201 (with two domes), and very fine they looked in their bright new coat of green. The loco would return, much slower, about 3.15 p.m., stopping at the station.

One day in June 1924, we were all silently listening to our headmaster's lecture, when I spotted a huge bright green shape slowly going by. This turned out to be "Remembrance' in its first coat of green paint with 'Southern B333" on the bunker. I was so excited I rose to my feet, and pointing out of the window, shouted out "Look!" Every head turned, including the master's. When it had passed he looked at me and said, "Come out". I went to the front of the class, he produced his cane and I received "six of the best" for causing a disturbance!

There was a "City Limited" from Worthing Central about 8.35 a.m. stopping at Hove, then straight up to London Bridge non stop. It came past the school about 8.45 a.m. and we always called it "the quarter to nine". A few of us every morning would walk up to the station about ¼ mile away, where a footpath ran alongside the north side of the railway line, which had a right hand curve in it as it approached the path. The express would come tearing down on us, whistle shrieking, usually with a "Baltic" tank on, but sometimes an "Atlantic", at about 60-odd, and the engine would seem to be "nosing" from side to side. The same cloud of dust and paper followed it as those on the main line. Having seen it, we'd run back to school.

I left this school at the end of the summer term, and started at Worthing High School for the September term.

This was hopeless for train spotting, as the line couldn't be seen from the school at all. It did have one consolation however. I had to go by train! Our train left Shoreham at 8.27 a.m. and always had two engines on. The usual suburban tank engine, plus a large express engine; a "B4X", "Atlantic" or "Bessborough", or "Abergavenny". Even Baltic tanks were used at times. They were most likely working out to West Worthing to take a later train up to London, and it was easier to send them out on this train, than arrange a separate path for them as a "light engine". The journey home was not so exciting, as we only had a small tank engine, and usually L.S.W.R. coaches, still in their "salmon pink". The train did however run non-stop, going through Lancing station in fine style!

If school finished early, the homeward trip was made on the "motor train", a Stroudly "D1" 0-4-2 tank, with two coaches on each end of it, and the driver in the first coach controlling the loco with compress air operated controls even to an

Radial Drills in Frame Shop.

The Big Steam Hammer in the Smiths Shop.

15

Interior of the Boiler Shop in the early 1900's.

The Southern Railway Company's first "PACIFIC" type locomotive No. 325 Abergavenny nears completion in Erecting Shop, 1910. Dan Hastings the author's future chargehand second from right.

16

air whistle! These motor trains had a fine burst of acceleration away from stations, when the driver felt like it.

Very soon I began to cycle to school, as it was more convenient. It did away with the long walk each end, to and from the station. This was about the time of the introduction of the "King Arthurs", and one would come tearing through Shoreham about 7.0 p.m. on a "down" commuter express. I used to cycle down to the bridge over the river to see this engine return about 8.20 p.m. in reverse, at the head of a goods train just trundling along. It was a fine way to take in the majesty of the King Arthurs, as it would be doing less than 20 m.p.h. and the movement of the rods working the valve gear could be observed with the greatest of ease.

The last type of engine to claim my attention during this period was Maunsell's ill-fated "K" class, or as they were better known, the "River" class 2-6-4 tanks. I first saw one of these about 1925 in the centre road of Brighton station, between platforms 2 and 3, when it was on its way to the shed and the turntable, after working a down "fast". It was quite a noisy beast too! The ejector was hard on, releasing the brakes, and when the driver opened the regulator, there was a loud "PLOP", which I learned later was the snifting valves closing. As it moved away the beats were loud and clear, which is more than could be said for some of the Brighton engines. It greatly impressed me, and gave an impression of great power.

I remember seeing the only three cylinder example No. A890, "River Frome", working through Shoreham fitted with indicator shelter on the front, to protect the men perched up on the front of it, taking the various readings. They were a very short lived class, and many lurid stories have been told by their crews of how they used to roll. After one came off the road near Sevenoaks in August 1927, the whole class were withdrawn, and converted to tender engines as detailed later.

My final phase of spotting took place some way from my previous activities, and this time, it was the G.W.R. main line to the West that claimed my attention.

The aunt in Somerset had moved from Burnham-on-Sea to Burnham (Bucks); or, as it was then called, Burnham Beeches. The back garden stretched down towards the line, and had a nice strong wooden fence at the bottom of the usual railway pattern of half round uprights, and three or four horizontal rails which was just right for sitting on!

My father visited her fairly regularly, and I always went with him. She kept a battered old pair of field glasses on a dresser, in her kitchen/diner so that even when I was in the house, I had a fine view of the locos through these glasses. I spent many hours sitting on that fence, and the sun always seemed to shine!

How beautiful those engines were I thought, with that lovely shade of green set off with the copper cap on the chimney, and the brass safety valve casing both well polished! The brass beading round the splashers, (and cabs of the later classes) also helped; and the tender, low sided, with the legend, GREAT WESTERN on its sides, and the Company's Coat of Arms in the centre, completed the picture.

All the express engines carried names, and with what relish they were recorded in the notebook. "North Star", "Shooting Star", "The Great Bear", (the largest and most powerful express loco in the country in its day), "Glastonbury Abbey", "Chaffinch", "Saint Bartholomew", "Lady Macbeth", "Cour de Lion", "Dorney Court", "Empire of India", "County of Devon", and the French Atlantic, "Alliance". Then in later years came "Caldicot Castle", "Windsor Castle", "King Richard I", and of course, the "K.G.V." or "King George V."

The thing that impressed me most with these G.W. engines was the ease with which they just seemed to glide along, albeit at great speed! There was none of the "Brighton roar" about them, or a great cloud of steam shooting up into the air. A thin wisp of white steam just along the coach tops. No smoke at all. The coaches seemed to make more noise than the engine, but the whole train seemed rock steady; none of the lurching and jumping about that I had seen on the "Brighton".

There was always an absence of fuss and smoky atmosphere about the G.W. Everything seemed to efficient. The chocolate and cream coaches looked superb, and they gave me a very comfortable ride.

The "Brighton" was always my favourite line, but the Great Western was a very close second!

One thing that I liked about the "Brighton". They had the smallest, and the largest tank engines in the country in the early 20's; and they were very fond of showing them either side by side, or one behind the other. To me, they looked most impressive!

Erecting Shop East Bay circa 1910 looking North.

Erecting Shop West Bay circa 1910.

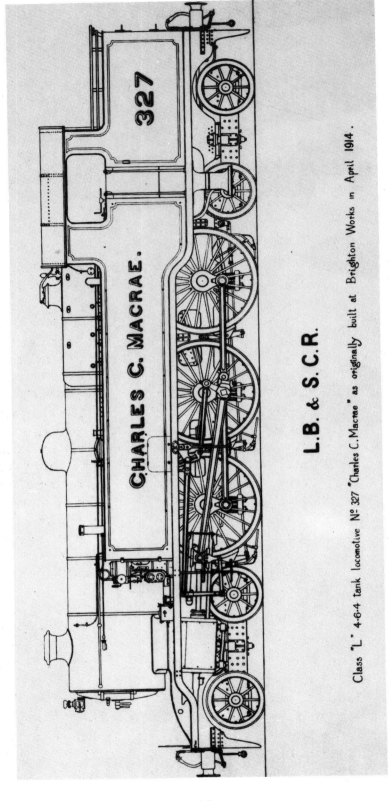

Broadside view of the Baltic tank in original condition drawn by Maurice Joly. The Weir feed pump ahead of the side tank was later moved inside the framing below the boiler.

Chapter Two

A Schoolboy goes to Work

I first made the aquaintance of Brighton Works on October 25th, 1928, when I started as a Premium Apprentice (taken on a month's trial) at the princely wage of 9s. 8d. per week. Upon completion of my month's probation, my father was required to pay the premium of £60 (approximately £12 for each year). Although the Southern Railway had been in existence for over five years, the L.B.S.C.R. carried on much as it had always done, and all the Brighton engines were under repair there.

On my first day I was a very raw recruit, as I had never previously been inside a factory of any sort! I was taken to the machine shop and turned over to the care of Chargeman Ginger Andrews. This character, I was soon to learn, was notorious throughout the works for the smell of his feet, particularly in the warm weather! I was put on the nut facing machine, which was just a mandrel with a 3-speed cone pulley, driven from the lineshaft via fast and loose pulleys. Various sized Whitworth Arbors could be inserted in the taper at the business end, and a "black" nut placed on it. Then with an ordinary compound slide rest, they were faced true and to size with a carbon round-nosed tool. Finished nuts were bagged up and taken to the Stores; mostly $1/2''$, $5/8''$ and $3/4''$ Whitworth.

Needless to say I did not find this very exciting, but was kept on it until the next apprentice arrived about a month later, when I had to show him how to work it, and then I was transferred to the "Bolt ending" machine, a slightly more complicated edifice which "topped and tailed" bolts of the excrescence left at both ends for the "centres", as they were all turned between centres by the turners, and centres removed by me afterwards! It was certainly better than the first effort, but still not very exciting!

Whilst on this machine I was nearly deafened by some very heavy, continuous hammering, coming from the erecting shop only a few feet away across the gangway. There seemed no end to it so I decided to investigate. I found two frame plates set up vertically and a gang of men trying them over with long straight edges. When they came to a hollow, they marked it with chalk and then the labourers pounded away with sledge hammers at it, until the chargeman was satisfied it was as straight and true as he could get it. It took several days of this treatment to get both frames O.K. and I wondered how the men's ears survived this racket! Upon enquiring further I was told that these frames were for the new "Z" class 3 cylinder shunting engines, eight of which were going to be constructed at Brighton, using our "C2X" boilers, but were going to be numbered in the "A" prefix series, 950 to 957. (This I thought to be rather unfair on Brighton Works as they should have had a "B" prefix!)

These were the last new engines constructed at Brighton Works prior to World War II and I watched their progress with interest. I made periodic visits to the shop to see how much progress had been made. It seemed painfully slow to me! However, the first one was at long last completed, and I made a point of being out in the yard on the bridge to watch it depart for the first time under its own steam. It struck me at the time that a very large amount of rusty water came out of the cylinder cocks when she was given steam. The other seven followed at intervals, always preceeded by the racket described above on their frames, but I was further away from it by then, so it wasn't so bad.

During this winter of 1928–29 there was very little heating in the machine shop. On starting work at 8.0 a.m. (by this time I had been shifted on to a "Capstan" making nuts from hexagon bar), the first job was to thaw out the frozen suds pump by putting a piece of burning oily waste on it. The tray and sump of the machine were dealt with by visiting the Smith shop and coming back with a large lump of red hot scrap iron and dumping it in the frozen sump!

If you had not set fire to the pump belt in the defrosting described above, after priming the pump, you were ready to start work. The foregoing antics would have consumed about one hour of valuable time, and very soon it was time for "lunch" – a sandwich in newspaper and a cuppa from a flask. A de-luxe version was to re-visit the Smithy for a new helping of hot iron, and then place the "sandwich" on the iron for a few moments which turned it into toast. Black as a cinder outside but raw inside!

The stop for lunch was unofficial, and had to be made with one eye open for the foreman, and if you heard "eye-up" from next down the line you knew he was about and lunch had to be hidden until he had gone. The chap behind me, on the nut tapper, was required to roll up his sleeves and work in a bath of water-based suds as the nuts were completely submerged in holders below suds level. It was so cold that the suds kept turning to ice, and as the poor bloke was on piece work, we used to take it in turns to run down to the Smithy for lumps of hot iron for him to thaw out the suds! After each stop of this nature it would be necessary for me to re-prime the suds pump on my machine on re-starting, and it might take a quarter of an hour to get that pump working again, so you can imagine that the production rate was not very high.

Brighton's largest and smallest tank engines pose together in the
loco. yard circa 1914.

"Z" class shunter No. A950, the last type of New engine built by Brighton works prior to World
War II stands with E3 class tank No. 453, still in "Brighton" livery six years after the grouping,
outside Ashford works 1929.

23

Part of Machine Shop showing belts and shafting.

Dealing with a "hot box" on Brighton Running Shed.

Even worse off was poor old Jack Burfield working (in turn) two bolt screwing machines. The dies were fed with neat whale oil, which not only had an unpleasant smell, but could not be warmed up with the hot scrap iron as could the water based suds. At the far end of the machine shop was a sizeable surface grinder which could take six slide valves at a time on its table. It also had a magnetic holding device for ferrous jobs and I well remember one day it was grinding merrily away when there was a power failure. All the machinery began to slow down and as soon as the job came into contact with the grinding wheel above, having now no "hold", it was lifted bodily from the table and hurled through a wooden partition into the erecting shop next door. Luckily no one was hurt.

Smoking was not permitted in the works, so when a "drag" was desired it was necessary to "go below" with the paper, to "pick out the winners". The loo consisted of a long wooden trough with a wooden edge which the attendant used to scrub to a "snowy" white. He would make periodic inspections to see that no one was sitting there without his trousers down! Woe betide anyone who was so caught, as he would be made to de-bag in no uncertain manner. Old Bert, the attendant, didn't want dirty overalls on his white woodwork. In spite of being very spartan loo accommodation by modern standards, the place was kept scrupulously clean!

Outside the brass shop was a battery of "Stirk Veloplanes", the tables of which would take about four driving axle-boxes end to end. They were belt-driven from the lineshaft, in one direction by an "open" belt and in the reverse direction by a "crossed" belt. The operators were very skilled in setting up these machines to earn maximum piece work. The weight of the moving table and four axle-boxes was considerable, and they would so position their direction changing stops as to change over little more than halfway down the stroke. The inertia of the table and job would carry it the rest of the stroke once the machine had worked up to full speed, in spite of the squealing coming from the belt trying to drive it in the opposite direction. They could so arrange things that the belt slip would just overcome table inertia just after the tool had completed its cut and likewise the return stroke. In this fashion they could make the job pay well. The strain on the belts working in this fashion was terrific and breakages were not unknown. If this occured on the return stroke there was nothing to stop the table, and it would continue until it crashed into the wood partition separating the brass and machine shops. The latter bore many scars gained in these circumstances. I never heard of anyone being injured, luckily.

Before I leave the machine shop, mention should be made of a very large character by the name of Tom Hefferan, called by us boys Tom Elephant! He always wore a battered old trilby, and as he bent over his vertical slotting machine working the handles, he was either chewing tobacco and spitting it out at intervals, or singing at the top of his voice! In passing it is worth noting that during the whole of my time at the loco I never once saw a micrometer used in the machine shop. Most of the men didn't even know what it was, let alone how to read it! I'm not suggesting that the limits worked to were the same as in the Rocket/Computer age, but those old craftsmen relied on the "feel" of their callipers, and they were surprisingly accurate. "Mikes" may possibly have been used in the Toolroom, but it's one place that I never worked in.

Even old Tom Harrington, turning up bronze spheres for clack valves, did them all "free-hand" with a scraper knocked up from an old file. When the finished clack boxes (mainly for I3 class tanks) were tested under 350 lbs. hydraulic, very little passed by those ball valves!

As my machine shop training was not to be very extensive (I was a Fitter's Apprentice), during the Spring of 1929 I was told to report one morning to Harold Ward, chargeman of one of the brass shop benches. There is an old and very true saying, "You can't please everybody", and I certainly couldn't please this man. He seemed to take an instant dislike to me and I can't say that I was overjoyed with him! In fairness to him though I must say that he did give me a turn on all the jobs that the gang did. These consisted of packing water gauge columns, and test cocks, and ultimately putting them on test and getting them passed by the Stores Inspector, on the air main at 100 P.S.I.; facing up flanges, and then hydraulic testing, clack boxes for the various Stroudley classes, which were still fitted with crosshead pumps. Then there was tapping out washout caps with a 3″, II T.P.I. tap!

The summer of 1929 was a very hot one and the brass shop had a glass roof as did all the works. A gang of men used to come round and whitewash the outside of the roof to keep the heat within bounds. By the time they got to us the summer was nearly over!

However, I had the job of pulling this 3″ tap around and it required a big spanner with a 3 ft. length of tube on it and sometimes a big tommy bar in that when the tap got well in! I used to sweat like a pig on that job! Another hot one was sweating together various half bushes for the turners to bore out. They were mainly neck rings for valve spindle and piston rod glands. A gas fire on the bench warmed them up (and the operator), and when hot enough they had to be treated with a Sal-ammoniac block dipped in killed Spirits of Salts, then the solder applied. One half was then placed on top of the other in the vice and a heavy weight put on it. Whilst it set as it cooled down, you pushed on with the next one.

We also fitted new neck rings in the tail rod covers and tested these under hydraulic pressure, faced up drivers' brake valves, (used in the front driving coach of a "motor" train), fitted new valves to and tested safety valves (hydraulic) and one man only (a Mr. Brown) repaired and tested pressure gauges. Every so often a super master gauge was inserted in the test rig and his

"L" class 4-6-4T No. 327's Boiler on "Iron Man" Riveter in the Boiler Shop circa 1914.

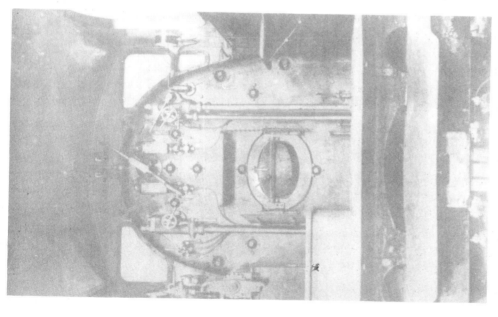

Cab view of a Brighton Atlantic as seen by the author on his first day in the Erecting Shop.

"Gladstone" No. 172 B1 class awaits scrapping in the East Bay Erecting Shop. 11-9-33. First engine worked on by the author.

Reg Cooper in the Erecting Shop in 1931, rests on a S.E.&C.R. "E1" class after his antics with black cotton across the doorway to the left of the third bench vice.

own master gauge which was used to set the repaired gauges was checked and if necessary adjusted.

I have already mentioned the heat in this shop, and one stifling day in early August, it was more than apprentice Harry Felton could stand. He hit on the brilliant idea of taking his trousers off and putting his boiler suit on without them! The first part of the operation went off quite well, but as soon as he had taken off his trousers, someone grabbed the boiler suit and ran round the benches with it, pursued by Harry, shirt tails flying! Shouts went up, others joined in the chase, one with an oil can. Harry was eventually cornered by the chap with the oil can and I leave you to guess what happened! Suffice to say that Harry never repeated this brilliant idea.

On Saturday afternoon, 24 August, 1919, I had the misfortune to get mixed up with a bull-nosed Morris Oxford whilst riding my motorcycle. This smashed up by left leg and I nearly had to have it amputated. I was off work for several months and it was mid-January 1930 when I went before the M.O. to see if I could resume work. He gave one look at the leg and nearly fainted! Even to this day it's got a double "set" in it, and is about ¾'' shorter than my right one.

He told me to come back in a fortnight. I did so, and this time he pronounced me fit for duty, for which I was very thankful, as I was getting bored stiff at home.

By the time I got back it was time for another shift for me. This time to the larger Brass Shop gang of Ted Smith. Although he had the reputation of being a "nigger driver" I got on very well with him and he seemed to like me. In fact, I can honestly say, that of all the men I came in contact with in the works, Harold Ward was the only one I couldn't get on with and who didn't like me.

Having now resumed after my several months' absence, everything was changed. Although I still "clocked on" at the same clock I had used since my first day, under the machine shop office, which was perched up in the air so that the foreman could see what was going on all around the shop, my number was changed, making the third I'd had since my start.

There were three brass shop benches, one under the control of Harold Ward, already referred to, and the other two under Ted Smith. All had vices on both their long sides and men or boys working one to a vice. My new home was only inches away from the old one, but I faced the opposite direction. Along the far end of all three benches ran the compressed air testing rig for the Stores Inspector to pass the various fittings after repair, before they could be accepted by the stores.

This gang did all the larger and heavy fittings, injectors, vacuum brake ejectors, sight feed lubricators, etc., of the *brass* cab fittings. They also did bulk orders for a host of small fittings, and I was one of a number of boys put on the assembly of water drain valves, for the steam heating pipes for the coaches.

29

Smith had a very large order for these, and they were required urgently. A mountain of component parts was heaped on our bench, and we had to assemble the ball valves, and put red lead paste (like putty) on the caps holding the balls in. During the morning, Ted would come round to see how each one was faring, and those who were getting on with the job and not just larking about, would be told to "work dinner hour".

This meant that when everyone else knocked off at 12.30 p.m. we carried on. One of the lads not working would be detailed to call in at Mepham's Bakers shop, on the corner of New England Road, and bring each of us back a bag of assorted cakes as he came back to work. Seven cakes for sixpence we got, and the lads christened them "bags o' wind". We devoured these as we worked at the bench, and in spite of the fact that the red lead was applied with our fingers, I never heard of anyone suffering from lead poisoning! About 4.00 p.m. Ted would come round and hand out the "pass outs" to be given up to the watchman at the gate at 4.30 p.m. Otherwise no was allowed to leave until the hooter went at 5.30 p.m. This was greatly sought after by the lads, as they finished an hour earlier, without loss of pay, and Ted got an extra hour's production, as others took over from us from 4.30 to 5.30 p.m.

Ted did nothing himself except supervise, plus all the paper work for the entire gang; unlike his opposite number, Harold, who was always working on some job or other himself, when he wasn't booking up. If Ted saw anyone at any time not actually working, he would shout at him to get on with it. Hence his reputation as a "nigger driver". In spite of this, I found him quite a likeable chap. If you carried on with your work, you had nothing to fear from him. He knew the ones to keep his eye on and shout at!

At the end of the day, we all washed up in an ordinary bucket of hot water, which the boys took it in turn to fetch from a trough, just inside the erecting shop door. About 5.15 p.m. the duty boy would take the bucket of old soapy water, throw it away down the drain under the trough, fill his bucket from the trough, and return it to the big iron tray used for safety valve testing. This tray would catch any overspill from the bucket during washing. The trough got its hot water from first being filled three parts cold water, by one of the erecting shop labourers; a pipe in the bottom of the trough was coupled up to the main steam pipe of a vertical boiler, just outside the door. Steam was then turned on, condensing in the water, and rapidly warming it up.

Now the more artful of us used to empty the old water down a drain under a fire hydrant, near the end of the brass shop gangway, instead of the trough's drain. This meant the bucket was empty for the second half of the outward journey. Now the lad who tested the safety valves, Les Pierce, would, when a new recruit was "on the bucket", tip most of the water out into the big tray, and put in its place, his 56 lb. testing weight! The remaining water just covered this,

30

The Works from Preston Circus looking west.

4-6-4T Stephenson, overruns the turntable and knocks the wall down into New England Road, after working the down "Southern Belle" 30-9-22 about 1.00 p.m.

A corner of the Boiler Shop.

Boilers in store outside Boiler Shop.

and being pretty thick and dirty, the weight was invisible. If the "bucket boy" made a grab at it, to pick it up as he passed, as most of us did, the effect would be to pull the boy virtually to the ground, as in effect the bucket seemed "bolted to the ground".

Now all of us had had this trick played on us, but upon recovering one's stance, the obvious thing to do was to remove the 56 lb. weight, and proceed with a nigh empty bucket! One lad named Bill Ramsey was not quite so smart, and would fall for any old gag. He'd been sent all over the place for such things as "glass hammers", and "red oil for rear lamps". Each chap he asked would keep a straight face, and send him along to someone else! I've known him be gone for over an hour on some "wild goose" chase, and then be none the wiser that he was being "taken for a ride". One evening it was Bill's turn for the bucket, and he rushed up to grab it: unknown to him, Les had placed the weight in position. He finished up on the floor amid roars of laughter. Not to be outdone, Bill picked himself up, grinning all over his face, lifted the bucket *and the weight inside it*, and staggered down all the way to the trough with it. Everyone in the shop (including old Ted Smith) were splitting their sides with laughter; but they still hadn't seen the best bit to come! Arrived at the trough, Bill removed the weight, after having emptied the small amount of water covering it, filled his bucket, then commenced his return journey with the bucket in one hand, *and the 56 lb. weight in the other*! As he passed through the lines of machines, each of the turners gave a cheer, and by the time he reached his goal, the whole brass and machine shops were cheering loudly. It amazed me to find that after it was all over, Bill was laughing about it as much as anyone!

Another favourite, this time when washing up, was for someone to say they'd dropped half-a-crown in the bottom of the bucket, and would you get it for them, as they'd dried their hands. This meant there was more steam than water in the 'mixture", and most of us were wise to it, and would say we'd get it in the morning. Bill, however, nearly scalded himself one day, searching for it!

The bench was equipped with a coal gas supply, and a compressed air supply both with their own control cocks. We used to use this as a high powered blowlamp, as we had a collection of gas fittings comprising a tee, and two elbows, resembling a letter "H" with "half a leg" missing, and fed by two flexible pipes coupled up to the aforementioned control cocks. The compressed air one was very hard to turn, and one day our friend Bill (of bucket fame), had been using the blowlamp, and duly turned off the gas. The air cock defied him however, so he just stood there, holding his hand over the end of the pipe! He had been there some minutes, when old Ted spotted him, and bellowed out, what the so-and-so did he think he was doing! When Ted heard the reason for him standing motionless, with his hand over the pipe's end, trying to contain 100 lbs. per square inch, he didn't know whether to laugh, or explode into one of his bouts of swearing at him. He did however, turn off the air, thus releasing Bill. The reader would do well to remember the name of Bill Ramsey, because it will crop up time and again in this story. If there was anything stupid that could be done, you could be sure that Bill would do it!

The method employed at Brighton was for each apprentice to go through the various shops, spending a certain time in each. If, for instance, Bill Brown started three months after Jim Green, then he would follow him round always three months behind! This did not apply to machinists, or turners' apprentices, as they alone did not move out of the machine shop. All pupils, premium apprentices, and ordinary apprentices (the latter confined to sons of Railway employees), went first to machine shop, then brass shop, then either erecting shop or fitting shop. Here all the large bits and pieces, such as reversing shafts, coupling and conn. rods, eccentrics, axle boxes, expansion links, reversers (screw or lever) etc. etc. were attended to. After this, some time would be spent with the millwrights, and some with a leaning to close limit fitting and machining would go to the tool room.

There was also the Drawing office, where all premium apprentices were supposed to spend about three months, which unfortunately I never did. I was lucky enough during my stay at the works, just to get in on the "last one" of any particular job to be executed at Brighton Works. By the time I was ready for the Drawing office, my luck had run out. It was already closed down! My greatest friend, fellow premium apprentice Henry Parrott, who was about two months in front of me, was not satisfied with this, and saw the Works Manager, Mr. Gardiner, about it. Mr. Gardiner said there was nothing he could do about it as the Drawing office was defunct. Nothing daunted, Henry decided to write to the C.M.E., Mr. R. E. L. Maunsell, suggesting a transfer to Eastleigh, to get Drawing office experience. The C.M.E. compromised by transferring him to Lancing Carriage Works for three months. As he went over the head of the Works Manager to get his wish, his reward for this at the end of his apprenticeship, was to get his notice one week early, to leave on the day his apprenticeship terminated! Everyone else got their notice on the day they finished, so got an extra week in, working out their notice, at journeyman's rate.

I should explain here, that about two years after I started at the works no more apprentices were taken on, as the works were being "run down", and as I have already said, I was lucky enough just to scramble in on the "last one done in the works" of most jobs. Our last recruit, by the name of Knowles, a nice chap, whose Christian name I'm afraid I've now forgotten,* was even transferred completely to the Eastleigh Works, as it was considered he would not get sufficient engineering training at the works, in its closing down condition.

* Subsequently revealed as Roger.

However, to return to Ted Smith and the brass shop: I had now been with him for my "allotted span". I'd been on a variety of jobs, and learnt quite a bit, and developed quite a liking for old Ted. Our week started on Thursday morning, and one Wednesday afternoon in the late spring of 1930, the office boy handed me a letter. I could guess what it was going to tell me. It was hard to open it for the excitement that I felt! At last I got it open! I was to report to Mr. Worsley, the erecting shop foreman at 8.0 a.m. on the morrow. My first hand contact with the STEAM LOCOMOTIVE was about to BEGIN! I told Ted about it right away. He received it coldly. "Ah!" he sighed, "they always do that to me. They always go and take the best ones away, and leave me with the lazy so and so's!" Still, he wished me luck and said I could always go and see him if there was anything in his department I wanted to know about! How different I thought, from my departure from my previous gang across the way. I spent the rest of the afternoon packing up my effects for transfer the next day.

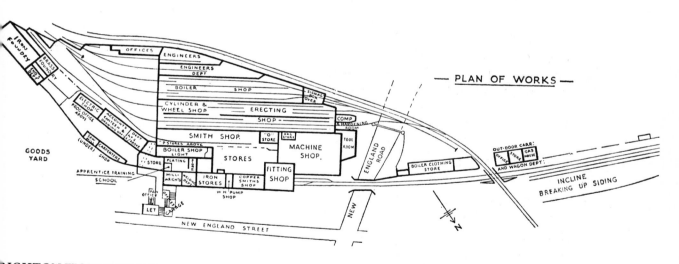

— PLAN OF WORKS —

BRIGHTON WORKS IN 1945

In the author's day, the Coppersmiths were over the New England Road Bridge, and there was no Apprentice Training School. "Boiler Shop light" was the Wheel Shop Stores and the Electric Shop, Canteen and Drawing Office, etc. was the Wheel Shop Proper (and Cylinder Shop). The Canteen was at the left hand side of the entrance in New England Street. The Boiler Shop went into the adjoining "Engineers' Dept."

which only had one building then, and there was no signal box there until electrification. The hardening room was a "Bosh" containing caustic soda cleaning tanks. The Smith Shop also was much bigger, taking in what is now "stores". There were several other detail changes impossible to show on this small plan.

(Published by kind permission of British Rail.)

Front elevation (section) of L class Baltic tank No. 327. Cab view (section) as new in 1914.

Chapter Three
The Erecting Shop with "Mad Jack"

At 8.0 a.m. on the Thursday morning, after having previously collected my "booking on ticket" from the Time office at the top of the steps up from New England Street, (the only entrance Works employees were allowed to use in those days; more about this later on), I presented myself to Mr. Worsley in the "Holy of Holies", the Erecting Shop Office.

Now I always held this man in high esteem. All the Works staff above the rank of chargeman wore bowler hats and no overalls, just their ordinary suit, and in the winter of course, their overcoat, as it was so jolly cold in the Works. Not only was Mr. W. so dressed, but he alone of all the foremen that I had seen, wore brightly polished *brown shoes*! They stuck out like "sore thumbs" in that motley collection of mostly old oily ex-Army boots of the 1914–18 war vintage, which left the service of His Majesty at the same time as their present wearers!

He looked at the letter I held out for his inspection. Without getting off his high office stool he just told me to report to chargeman Arthur Peake "in the far bay". I made my way to the far bay, and asked who "Arthur Peake" was. One of the fitters pointed to a short figure in grimy blue overalls, covered by an equally grimy blue jacket. A bushy moustache, waxed at the ends, covered the upper lip, and the head was covered with a huge, dirty, cloth cap.

So I made my first acquaintance with my next chargeman, one of the most likeable characters that I was to meet during my stay at the Works. He looked up at me, his blue eyes meeting my brown ones. "What's your name?" "Perryman," I said. He wrote it down on a dirty pad he carried in his pocket. "And your first name?" "Bert," I said. Again he scribbled on the pad. Then, "I want you to go over and work with Jack over there." He pointed to a towering figure, at present leaning up against the bench.

I went up to Jack and said, "I'm your new mate." He eyed me suspiciously. "They've just taken my mate away from me," he said. "Old Darky was a bloody good mate. If you turn out half as good as him, you'll do!" "What's your name?" he snapped. "Bert," I said.

He led me to a "B1" Gladstone, standing in the centre road. His late mate and he had almost finished its "general repair". It was the very last Gladstone to have a "general" at Brighton, number 172, and is pictured in this book standing in Brighton Erecting Shop East, II September 1933, awaiting scrapping. "Get up on top of the cab roof; where the stanchions come through, you'll find two large nuts. Tighten them up with a hammer and chisel. You know how to use a hammer, I suppose?" "Yes," I said. "Righto then, up you go." I scrambled up via the donkey pump, handrail, and firebox crown and saw my objectives. They had several gashes on them, from previous attacks by the same tools. I commenced operations, and after several blows, succeeded in dealing my left hand a severe blow, instead of the chisel! After I had recovered from the momentary shock that the blow gave me, I saw blood was pouring out of the gash. I decided evacuation was the best policy, so made my way below, to where Jack was awaiting me, having been watching me all the time. He eyed me with disgust. "Thought you could use a hammer," he jeered. "So did I," I said. "Seems as if I shall have to teach you starting at the bottom," he slung at me. "Anyway, off you go down the ambulance room and get that hand fixed." I did as I was told, and the M.O. fixed it up for me.

When I got back Jack had been up and tightened the nuts up himself. We didn't do much more that morning, as my hand was giving me a good deal of pain and Jack probably knew that. There were only a few odd jobs to do on the B1, which he attended to whilst I watched. He was waiting for his next engine to come in. He didn't make much conversation, and I could sense that I was a poor substitute for the late "Darky". (Biles was his name, and Arthur the handle.) He was as dark as a South African, very quiet, and slow speaking, and quite a nice chap really. Obviously Jack felt his loss very deeply.

Dinner time eventually came round and I hied me downstairs to the messroom, then situated at the bottom of the steps in New England Street. I sat down with my fellow apprentices who eyed my damaged hand. "Where are you working now?" "Erecting shop," I said. "Whose gang?" "Arthur Peake's," I replied. "And who's your mate?" one asked. "A big chap, named Jack," I said, as I didn't know his surname. The others exchanges glances among themselves. "God help you," said one. "You're with old 'Mad Jack'." "He works all his mates to death." "You'd better watch out. If you've taken half your hand off in your first morning, he'll have you in your box in a fortnight." My spirits sank at this. My enthusiasm for the erecting shop, so high at 8.0 a.m., began to evaporate rapidly.

I made my way back upstairs, collecting my brass "ticket" en route from the time office. A huge ledger reposed in here, and the time clerk had to enter all the

38

numbers booked in, morning and afternoon. A hooter blew at 1.20 p.m., and another at 1.27 p.m. Last one was at 1.30 p.m. and the hatch was then closed. Anyone after that was booked "late", and lost ¼ hour or ½ hour as the case may be. Same state of affairs existed in the mornings. Anyone not in by 8.30 a.m., i.e. ½ hour late, would not be allowed in until the afternoon shift.

I strolled up the centre road of the East Bay erecting shop; arriving at the "crossing" which was a sort of "minor road" running at right angles, and starting at the fitting shop, going through the machine shop, then across both East and West bays of the erecting shop, right through to the boiler shop. I turned my back on the stairs leading up to the foreman's office, down which I had come so excitedly only a few short hours before, to make my way back to the West bay and "Mad Jack". I wasn't looking forward to it a bit now. I'd be glad when 5.30 p.m. got round!

Then it happened! As I strolled leisurely across that crossing, just killing time, my eyes settled on the great bulk of H2 Atlantic No. 422, "North Foreland", which had entered the shops only that morning, and had evidently been placed in this berth whilst I was busily engaged knocking my hand about. Injuries and "Mad Jack" were instantly forgotten. I was alongside the step leading up into the cab. The handrail seemed naturally to attract my good hand. In less time than it takes to tell, I was up the step and inside the cab! For the first time in my life, I was in the cab of a Brighton Express engine, and of course, I had soon grabbed the regulator handle and opened it up. I fancied myself as a Brighton top link driver, taking the "Southern Belle" out of Victoria, and heading for the 1 in 64 up Grosvenor bank on to the bridge.

"How tough those drivers must have been to be able to shift that reverser," I thought. "I can't budge it, even with no steam on!" I did not know then, that the reverser was power-assisted by air frm the Westinghouse reservoir, via a servo motor. Even if I couldn't notch up, no matter. We were in full gear anyway (luckily forward), and the fireman would have to shovel a bit harder that's all. I might even have to help him if he tired, so I opened the firehole door to see how easy it would be! A loud bang greeted my efforts, followed by much clattering and several lesser bangs, whilst a cloud of rusty dust ascended steadily upward from the firehole. Although the shed firelighters had removed the firebars, prior to 422's visit to the shops, they had forgotten the baffle which directed air downwards from inside the door, down on to the firebed. My opening the door dislodged it, and it fell through the firebox, hit the rails on top of the pit, then down into the bottom of the pit, over which we were standing.

"What the hell do you think you're up to?" came a voice at the back. I turned round to see "Mad Jack" scowling at me from floor level. "Come on down out of it, and get to work with me; we're late starting as it is. Good job I came looking for you, or there's no telling what you might have got up to." My reign as a top link driver was over all too soon, but it was very exhilarating whilst it lasted!

I felt ready for anything that Jack might put me to. We didn't do much more that day, just a few odd jobs finishing off 172. But I had arrived in *the* shop; 422 just round the corner in the East bay was a wonderful tonic for me, just when I needed it. For many days afterwards, if ever I got despairing, I always fancied myself back on that footplate, fetching the "Belle" up out of Victoria! Of course before many days, little remained of 422 intact. The fitters were stripping her down for a general repair, but she had served her purpose as far as I was concerned.

That's how, when I built my first miniature locomotive fifteen years later, it turned out to be a 3½″ gauge Brighton H2 Atlantic. Its number? You guessed correctly. It was 422!

The reader will by now realize, that, in spite of high expectation on my part, my introduction to the erecting shop had not quite gone according to plan. This state of affairs however, did not last long. I soon found out that my mate, "Mad Jack", was so named, and was not all that popular among his workmates, because of his appetite for work! Anything that stood between Jack and him discharging his duties was removed or circumvented. He was an Irishman, Quinlivan by name, I learned. He stood about 6 ft. 3 ins. and was broad with it. Possessed of great physical strength, and more than ordinary endurance, he could really get on with it. That's why he had the reputation of working all his mates to death. I myself was approaching 6 ft., and then in my prime, also had quite an amount of strength; although I couldn't match Jack, who was approaching his thirties, and probably at his zenith of strength. He soon found out his new mate was eager to work and learn all he could and we went ahead rapidly.

Another thing helped our relationship. Jack was one of the very few men in the works, at that time, who held a driving licence. He rode a model 18 Norton, 490 c.c. with sidecar! I myself was interested in motor-cycles, and had a 249 c.c. Rudge-Whitworth with J.A.P. engine, at that time. In leisure moments between shifts, or when held up for materials, we would often have a discussion on motor-cycles. I also learned that one of his previous mates, Winton, also had a 493 c.c. New Hudson.

The erecting shop was served by two overhead travelling cranes of 35 tons capacity each. The west bay ones made by Vaughan & Sons, and the east bay by Craven Bros. Besides the main 35 ton lift, which was used when lifting complete engines, or boilers, there was a secondary lift capable of handling about 10 tons, which of course was much faster than the main lift. When we wanted to lift axleboxes, for bedding the boxes to the journals, we had to have the crane overhead the whole time. When anyone else wanted to lift anything heavy, say put on a chimney, etc., they had to wait for the crane.

2007, a rebuilt I1X 4-4-2T in the mid 1930's.

The works shunter outside the North end of the works standing on the bridge spanning New England Road circa 1930.

A busy scene in the Boiler Shop circa 1912.

The Wheel Shop, note the large lathes on the left, for machining them.

Now Jack and I were working on a 0-6-2T E4 Radial. We were hung up for stuff coming back from the machine and fitting shops. Not to be outdone, Jack decided to refit the front buffers, and sent me off to get the crane. The crane driver said he was busy with another gang working on axleboxes, and would not be available for an hour or more. When I told Jack this, he was not prepared to wait that long, or do anything else. He decided that *he* would lift up the buffer! I was instructed to stand by with a pointed tommy bar, and poke it through one of the top bolt holes of the bolting flange on the buffer stock. "When I lift," said Jack, "be ready to poke that bar through the hole, and for God's sake don't miss; as I'll only be able to hold it up just long enough for you to line it up," Jack lifted up the buffer by putting his arm right round it like a cradle, and by the greatest of good fortune, I was able to poke the bar through the holes the instant Jack was high enough. The second buffer was dealt with in like fashion, after we'd bolted up the first one, thus freeing the tommy bar. I don't think there was another fitter in the works either strong enough, or mad enough, to emulate Jack's method!

Another of our jobs was to try the axleboxes up in the horns, after the machine shop had machined the new liners, fitted by the fitting shop. For this, the boys had to hunt round the shop and gather up sufficient wood packing blocks of various shapes and sizes, ranging from 12" × 12" about 2 ft. long, to small segments which had once done duty in the carriage wheels, as wood filling between centre and tyre. Pit boards would also be needed, three for a six coupled engine, and two for a four coupled. Each board spanned the pit, between the piers supporting the rails, and the boy stationed himself in the pit, whilst the fitter was outside the engine, with a wooden pole 8 to 9 ft. long, round at the handle end, square at the "business' end. This was placed through the appropriate rung of an axlebox "horse", a sort of steel ladder, and the box lifted up into the horns. The "boy" placed packing under the box, whilst the fitter took a new bite on the next rung up for the next lift. When high enough, the "boy" put the hornstay into position, and this supported the box. The wedges or liners (according to type of loco) would then be adjusted, so that the box would hold itelf in any position, between right up and right down.

After all the boxes had been so treated, we would put "false centres", consisting of any suitable length of scrap strip steel, jammed in the box. This was carefully centre-punched to record the true centre of the driving axlebox, and then trammels obtained from the toolroom, for the class of loco under repair. The centres of the other boxes would then be marked out with the trammels, from the driving centre. Upon completion of this, the axleboxes would be removed, and a labourer would wheel them round to the axlebox turner in the machine shop. He would set them up true to our centres, and then bore out the boxes to suit the axle journals. The turner would visit the erecting shop with his

43

callipers, and take journal sizes for each box. Upon their return to us, we would then, with the aid of the crane, bed them (with scrapers made from old files), to the axle journals. The boxes were then assembled with their springs on the journals, (in the case of the older types), ready for wheeling. The newer types with "J" spring hanger brackets had to have the springs put on separately *after* wheeling. The pit board and packing ritual would have to be repeated, on the big fellows; and on some of the six coupled classes (Baltic tanks in particular), it was very awkward on the trailers, owing to the proximity of the cross stretchers in front of the ashpan.

Wheeling an engine was quite interesting. The lifting gang would first come along and lift the two or three pairs of driving wheels, and (if applicable), the trailing pony truck for "I" class 4-4-2 tanks, "J" 4-6-2 tanks, and "E" class 0-6-2 tanks, on to the end of the centre road, which had a long pit built into it, on its end, just inside the big doors at the shop's end. The cranes would then be brought along to the loco, and the large lifting hooks placed under the buffer beams, or in shackles, attached to holes, especially made in the frames for the purpose, on the larger engines. The loco would then be lifted right up high (to clear all obstructions), swung over the centre road, then brought up the shop until it was over the wheels. The entire gang was mobilized, one to each axlebox, with chargeman Arthur Peake outside to give and take orders (to the lifters).

Starting on the leaders, the engine would be gently lowered, and fitters and mates had to guide the boxes into the horncheeks. If they got caught up, there were frantic shouts of "Whoa". As soon as both sides of the leading wheels were entered, the drivers were tackled; and lastly the trailers (if a six coupled); then the trailing pony truck (if fitted). Hornstays would then be bolted on. Spring hanger pins would be placed through the holes in the frames in the case of the older types; where the springs were placed on the axleboxes before wheeling. Whilst this latter operation was "on", chargeman Peake would keep bawling out, "Don't put your fingers in the hole. Use any metal rod you have handy." Somebody, sometime, had done so, and when the cranes lowered the loco, the chap lost his finger, sheared off in the springhanger! Bogies were never fitted to any engine at this stage, but the last thing, just before the engine was taken out of the shop to be steamed up.

Upon the engine being returned to its berth, the next thing would be to refit the coupling rods. On a four-coupled engine, this wouldn't be too bad. The worst would be an "Atlantic", because of the weight of the rod. Here again, the entire gang would be mobilized, for a six-coupled engine particularly. The whole rod had to be lifted at once, and when the bushes were in line with the crankpins, chargeman Arthur would push them on with his foot. Even the labourer, an artful old codger named Jack Mason, would be pressed in to help us. He would always take up station next to "Mad Jack", as he knew he would have but little weight to lift there. Jack however, was wise to this, and one day when we were putting the rods on a "Mogul", (about the worst one of the lot), Jack stationed me on the other side of Mason to himself. He had previously told me what he was going to do; then, as soon as the rod was up, Jack was going to cough, and momentarily stop lifting. I was instructed to do the same, so that the whole of the weight that the three of us had, would be transferred to Mason! Well, Jack duly coughed, and we let go. Mason went straight down on the floor under the weight, because as you can imagine, he was doing next to nothing. Jack was ready for this however, and had told me to lift like mad as soon as Mason went down. Up we went and straight on to the crankpin, before Mason has recovered. "There you are Peaky," Jack called out, "I told you he was only an ornament on this job. Take him away, and don't let him come near me any more. We manage better without him as he only gets in the way."

On this class (the K Mogul of L. Billinton's design), the rods had to start from the floor, about half their own length to the rear of their ultimate position, as the guide yoke supporting the slide bars passed right round underneath them. The rod had therefore to be lifted to its proper height, then everyone had to walk forward, and pass it through the guide yoke; the men on the leading end of it having to rest it on the yoke, whilst they ran round the front end to catch hold of it again, as it came through the yoke. Procedure was reversed when taking them off, which made them much more awkward then any other class, where the procedure was one man, (or boy), to a crankpin; prize them off the pins, and let them fall on to the wooden floor.

The unofficial lunch break was easier to take in the erecting shop than any other, the majority of the staff going up into the tank engine cabs for this, and shutting the doors. If the engine was stripped down to a large extent, we had to transfer to the nearest one that was more or less intact. The Brighton luckily possessed many more tank than tender engines, so there was always one available. Now if there was one thing that "Mad Jack" could not stand, it was half cold tea! Someone had made the tea, and Jack complained that it was cold. No one else could touch it, because it was too hot! An argument ensued, and Jack made a wager that he would drink it *boiling*! It was duly fixed up for the afternoon session. We had rubber pipes coupled every so often to the gas main running along the pits. In the end of the rubber was a short length of copper pipe flattened at the end. One of these was always passed up through the cab floor, and a metal billycan, holding about a quart of water, was suspended on a wire from any convenient fitting in the cab, whilst the gas jet played underneath it. As soon as the water boiled, the tea boy had a small piece of newspaper, containing the tea and sugar mixed together. Sometimes it even contained a few teaspoonfuls of condensed milk as well. In this instance, it was just tea and sugar, which was shot in as soon as the water boiled. Jack straight away, lifted the can with his bare hands, and took a jolly good mouthful of it, just as it was without any milk, and swallowed it! How he was able to do this without injury to himself, I never knew, but he seemed none the worse for it! Anyway he won his wager.

In order to even up the work he could get out of his gang Arthur Peake decided to shift us around after I had been with Jack for a few months. He sent me to work with a much older man named Bill, (I will withhold his surname for reasons which will be apparent later). Jack in return, had a young chap named James put with him. The latter was not very strong physically, and I could see that there would soon be trouble there, as he would not be able to stand Jack's pace of working! My new mate was nowhere near so strong as Jack, and I soon found out, nothing like as industrious either! Neither Jack nor I were at all happy with this change. He couldn't get on, as for long periods his young mate could do nothing, Jack having worked him to a standstill. I couldn't get on, as my mate was missing for long periods at a time, taking it easy.

I soon got fed up with this, and as I had had such good training with Jack, I knew what to do, and used to get on with it on my own. This suited Bill better still, and he was missing longer and longer! His work was getting done just the same, by me! One day I was sitting down in the pit, feeling pretty glum, waiting for Bill to come back to help me in a two-man job. Suddenly a face appeared in between the driving wheels; it was Jack! "Where's your —— mate?" he asked. "Don't know," I said. "I haven't seen him for some time," "What you're on," he asked. I told him, and said I had got as far as I could, on my own. He was horrified, and said it was not my place to do that, but my mate's, as he was responsible. Then I asked where Jack's mate was. He said he was sitting down "resting". "I also can't get on by myself," said Jack; "come on out of it and come up and help me." "What will Peaky say?" I asked him. "Never mind about him," says Jack. "He wants the work done; I must have a mate to help me do it." I stayed with Jack for the rest of the day, and although Peaky saw us, he didn't say anything. Jack was his favourite fitter. No wonder, as he turned out far more work than any of the others, and I suspect that had a lot to do with it.

The Frame Shop circa 1912. "H2" Atlantic frames in course of erection.

Turners at work on old "Craven Bros., Manchester" lathes.

STROUDLEY TANK ENGINES

"E Special"

"E1"

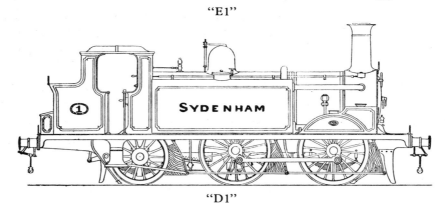

"D1"

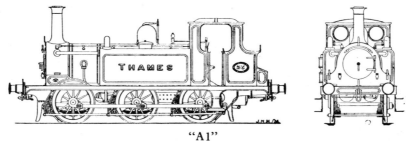

"A1"

48

Chapter Four

"Peaky"

"God made the bees
The bees make honey
Peaky does the work
and the gang gets the money."

This little rhyme I heard many times during my stay in the gang of which Arthur Peake was chargeman. I have already mentioned my impressions of him at our first meeting. I can now only repeat that he was one of the most likeable characters that I ever came across; not only on the Railway, but throughout my life.

I don't think I ever saw him really angry. He seldom said a cross word to anybody. If anybody had to be taken to task over anything, Arthur had a very nice way of doing it.

Very short of stature, and in a grubby old pair of blue overalls, with an equally grubby blue jacket (and large grubby cloth cap to match), he was about sixty when I first met him, and had been a long time with the Railway. He had been a shed fitter at New Cross Gate for a time, and often would amuse us with his tales about it.

He was renowned throughout the whole works and running sheds for his snuff box. All day long, men would come up to him and say, "Hello Arfur," and at the same time rubbing their thumb and first finger vertically up and down their overall. "Peaky" would produce his snuff box, open it up, and hold it up for his visitor to have a pinch. He never failed to have a pinch himself at the same time! Heaven knows how much he consumed during the week, but he fairly reeked of it; and it seemed to be running down his nostrils! I can honestly say that I was one of the few who never had any of it. The smell of "Peaky" was enough to turn me off it!

It was most amusing to me when we made one of our periodic visits to the Running Shed, to carry out some minor job that had been booked by the trial driver, whilst testing out one of our repaired locos. In front of me would be "Peaky", and alongside him "Mad Jack" about twice his height. Suddenly, from nowhere, one of the shed fitters appears, not having seen "Peaky" for some time. "Morning Arfur! You don't seem to grow much. Your arse is very near the

49

ground!'' At the same time the finger cleaning exercise was being vigorously pursued. Out came the snuff box, and all would partake of it (except me.) We would be stopped for some minutes whilst the old pals had a chat; then off we'd move only to be stopped again and again by the other fitters. Jack would get fed up with it after a very little while, find out where our engine was standing, and proceed to it with me. We had usually effected the necessary repairs by the time "Peaky" managed to get along!

Whilst on one of these trips, I was alone in the cab with the driver and fireman; even Jack had gone off to find one of his old pals! The job booked for us was a leaking wash-out cap joint. It was so slight that they hadn't even bothered to let the steam down, as they were so short of motive power. Instead, the engine already had its traffic orders, and the driver and fireman were preparing it for its turn of duty.

I knew the drill by now. The first thing to do was to get up in the cab, and make contact with whoever was working on the loco. Seeing about 120 lbs. of steam on the gauge, I asked the driver what I should do, as I had been sent to renew a leaking joint.

"Bloody well leave it alone,'' was the curt reply. "Some while ago we had the same thing happen, and the silly so-and-so sent over from the shops to do it, never bothered to say anything about it to anyone; or see if there was any steam! He just started to take the cap off. I just managed to look out of the window, as the cap was on its last thread, and I shouted to him to jump for it, on to the track. He did just that, luckily without hesitating, just as the cap blew off. It was eventually found somewhere up Dyke Road Way! Luckily the fire was out, but there was still a tidy head of steam. If the fire had been in, I might not even have been here now! It'll just have to be left until the engine's out of steam, on her next shed day. T'won't take the shed fitter long to sort that out. I ain't booking her unfit for dooty just for a —— silly little blow such as 'ers got now!''

Jack returned at this moment, and after a conference with the driver, decided that nothing could be done at this stage, so we made tracks back to the shops.

However, to return to "Peaky". Every day, even dark wet evenings, he would dig his enormous "turnip" watch out about 5.0 p.m., look at it, and say, "Well lads, I'm going out to see the 5.5 go up; coming out Bert?" Sometimes I'd go with him, if we weren't too busy. We'd walk out on to the bridge spanning New England Road, and watch the "King Arthur" just getting into its stride, past the sheds. He wouldn't say anything, but it was obvious from the expression on his face that he was enjoying it as much as any schoolboy "train spotter". He never bothered with any other train, not even the "Southern Belle", but I never remember him missing the 5.5 p.m.

One very wet November afternoon in 1930 (you could always tell when it was wet in the erecting shop, because the roof leaked in many places!) Peaky came up to the engine I was working on in a very agitated state. "Bert! Bert! want a job? Strip 330's cab! She's just come in on the centre road, and I've got her for a general repair. I'm putting you and your mate on her, when I can find him," he added tactfully. My mate at this time was Bill. I didn't need any second bidding. I gathered up my set of tools and was soon up in that huge cab. 330 was a 4-6-4 "Baltic" tank, all 98½ tons of her, the biggest class of express loco on the "Brighton". As it turned out, she was also the last "Baltic" to get a "general" at Brighton. All after that were sent to Eastleigh. I didn't see anything at all of my mate Bill for the rest of the afternoon. I wasn't worried as I was thoroughly enjoying myself in the cab. In next to no time (so it seemed) the works hooter was blowing 5.30 p.m. I hurriedly had to put my tools away and dash around the station as I was, and just managed to catch my train home.

The next day 330 was placed in one of our "berths", and my mate had shown up, so we made a fresh start. Peaky was kept very busy from now on as all the material had to be booked out for repair as we got it stripped out. He also had to go round to the various shops to see how his parts were getting on. Being a large express engine, it was wanted back by the traffic department as soon as possible.

We even worked evenings overtime on this one, the only one that caused me to do this throughout my career. Even "Mad Jack" and his mate were put on it as well, to get it out quickly. I remember Jack joking to me about it being too much for my mate Bill, so he (Jack) had had to be put on it to get Bill out of his muddle.

"Peaky" always fancied himself as a bit of a blacksmith. Every so often in the erecting shop, a forge was built. This was really a circular steel drum, very like a 25 gallon oil drum with a chimney leaving its centre at the top. The chimney then joined up with the down pipe carrying rain water from the roof to the drains. The bottom of the forge was level with the bench top, and air was supplied via a 1½" bore pipe, running back and coupling on to the very large air blower used to supply air to the blacksmith's forges in the smith's shop. The forge was lined with fire bricks.

At the slightest excuse, "Peaky" would have a bar of steel in his fire, getting red hot, and then bring it out to forge it into some shape or other, on a big block of steel, that he had bolted to the bench to do duty as an anvil. He made all sorts of little odds and ends that we needed, either as special tools to assist the work we did, or for the job in hand. Fuel was obtained from the nearest loco that had any in its bunker.

During the early 1930's, the old L.B.S.C.R. main lines were being electrified, and we were naturally keen to get the latest news of how it was progressing. All sorts of rumours were rife in the Works, but the most common one was that "they can't get through Balcombe Tunnel." This tunnel apparently was very wet, and did give some bother, but the changeover was duly made on 1 January 1933.

The first electric "Southern Belle" was due in Brighton at 12.00 p.m. and there was quite a small crowd from the Works out on New England Road Bridge to see it arrive, including "Peaky".

Although I had been out of his gang for some time, we immediately "teamed up" and waited expectantly. Just about three minutes to twelve, she came tearing down from Preston Park, and I have never before, or since, seen any train, steam or electric, go by the end of the sheds at the bat she was doing.

One bowler-hatted V.I.P. over the shed side of the track, jumped out towards the driver, frantically waving him down!

Someone suggested it would finish up on the Palace Pier, but of course it was Westinghouse braked, instead of the Vacuum of steam days. It must have stopped all right in the end, as we never heard a crash!

Just as everyone was preparing to go back to their respective places, old "Peaky" remarked drily, "Anyway, it proved one thing; they must have now got through Balcombe Tunnel". This of course raised a good laugh.

No. 329 Stephenson of the second batch, under construction September 1921. Main and bogie axleboxes on floor at front.

After 1931 the "Baltics" were sent to Eastleigh for repairs and had the cabs (and at first chimney and dome) removed to clear low bridges. 2332 has arrived to be converted to a tender loco.

2329 after conversion to a tender loco., from the 4-6-4 tank original form, circa 1934. The only one of the class ever to run from London to Brighton with a passenger train, as a tender engine 23-6-56.

53

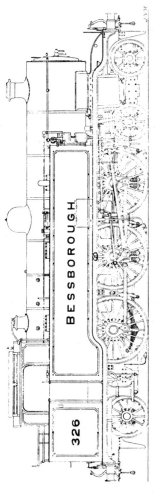

J Class 4-6-2 tank of 1912

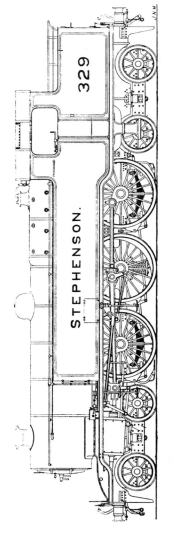

L Class 4-6-4 tank of 1922

L.B. BILLINTON EXPRESS LOCOS.

54

Chapter Five

Assorted Fun in the Erecting Shop

In the last chapter I mentioned about the hurry for 330. In spite of this, the job went on, and on, endlessly, it seemed. Bill said it was always the same on this class, they were too big for a fitter and his mate on their own. I pointed out to him that Jack and his mate had put in quite a bit of time on it, but Bill still said it was too big.

The traffic department was determined to have their loco back and, as it began to get near completion, the number of men working on it increased alarmingly. Coppersmiths and gasfitters were sorting their pipes out at the same time as we were doing our bit. To cap it all the foreman painter and his staff were drafted on to it, before we'd finished. They painted the top of the boiler, whilst my mate and myself were putting the dome and safety valve covers on. I never knew wet paint was so slippery. Only the large side tanks saved me from coming right down to floor level on several occasions! Somebody had clipped a lighted gas jet on to the handrail that ran outside the cab, and it swung round on to the new paint, setting it on fire!

The poor old painter nearly went mad over this. We had as much paint on us as the loco had on it. Our grimy foot marks were painted over many times on the boiler top. But at last all was finished and she eventually left the shops, even if she was several weeks overdue! I'm afraid the paintwork didn't look very pristine when she was sent out.

The engine was a thorn in our sides for weeks afterwards. Every few days "Peaky" would come up and shout, "Bill, 330 over the shed, drawing air in the smokebox." We'd draw out a new set of bolts and new brass dome nuts, and then go and knock out the old bolts, on some of which the nuts had actually melted, they'd been so hot, and replace them with the new set. I had one of the worst jobs of my whole life on this loco. When new, the Baltics were inclined to be a bit unsteady at speed, and it was thought that this was due to the large amount of water sloshing about in their large side tanks. Accordingly these tanks were cut

55

down in height; the Westinghouse brake pump was put down under the smoke-box, behind the leading bogie wheel, and the Weir feed pump just in front of the trailing bogie wheel. This pump now drew its water supply from a new horse-shoe shaped "Well tank" placed astride the driving axle, holding 450 gallons. There was an inspection manhole placed in the bottom of the front section.

Now the driver had reported that the Weir pump would not work. The pump fitter had been over and over that pump, but could find nothing wrong with it. He came to the conclusion that there was an interruption in the supply pipe. We were therefore detailed to examine the well tank. "Peaky" had consulted the drawings and discovered that although the suction pipe was bolted to the top of the tank, there was also an internal pipe bolted underneath this, running right down to the bottom of the tank.

Inspection of the tank's interior failed to establish this pipe's existence! It was missing! The coppersmiths were detailed to make a new pipe and then I had to get the upper part of me through the manhole, to fit it on. It had evidently been missing for some time, for the nuts would not go on those corroded studs.

"Peaky" saw the shed foreman and managed to borrow a dienut. I had to run this on the studs first, and had to work "blind" whilst leaning over backwards. I managed it at long last, but it was no picnic working in that wet confined space. It must have done the trick because we never heard any more about it, after I had refitted that internal pipe. I felt as if I had a permanent "set" in my back for weeks afterwards.

The demand to get the locos back to the traffic department when they were short of motive power, especially at holiday times, did sometimes have unfortunate results. Just before a Bank holiday the "Big Chiefs" carried out an inspection to see which locos they could rush through and get out for the holiday traffic. Several locos were marked as "probables". An "I3" 4-4-2 tank was one, so the paint gang came on as well as the fitters, and gave it a coat of "shop grey" till they could do it properly after the holiday panic. This one made it quite all right.

The last one of the probables was a "K" class Mogul, and this one was not so lucky. The cranes lifted it up and dumped it in the centre road over the pit. The fitters were trying to insert the yoke pins into a very obstinate brake gear.

The shunters had left it as late as they dared, it being the Saturday morning before the holiday. "Come on out from under there," shouted old Alf the shunter. "We're going to take her out in the yard." "Give us a few minutes more," yelled back the fitter, "we still haven't got the last yoke pin in."

The "Terrier" was now coupled on the back of the "Mogul" blowing off furiously. "Can't wait any longer," shouts Alf, "you'll have to finish her out in the yard. Drop down in the pit while we take her out." With that he blew his whistle and waved a green flag. The driver opened up the "Terrier", and it just about managed to get the still very stiff "Mogul" on the move.

Now there was a curve just outside the door, and it was uphill as well, so the "Terrier" was given all she could take. The two were going out in fine style, and the "Terrier" was now out in the open. Just as the "Mogul" was going through the door she must have lurched over a rail joint, which dislodged that obstinate yoke pin. Out it came and the brake rod slipped off the beam and dug into the floor.

A great cloud of smoke and steam issued forth from the "Terrier", but to no avail. The "Mogul" stopped half through the doorway, its brake gear immovably transfixed in the shop floor, which it had torn up for several yards! All efforts to shift the "Mogul" in any direction proved abortive. She was even out of range of the crane. Even the shop doors couldn't be shut! The poor old "Mogul" spent the holiday stuck in the doorway, with the doors closed on her as much as she would allow.

The brake rods had to be cut off with oxy-acetyene after the holiday, before she could be freed. Then new rods had to be made in the Smithy, so it was about another fortnight before she finally took the road.

Another casualty at a different time to the ones just considered, was a "J" class 4-6-2 tank. Again it was a case of rushing to get finished on a Saturday morning. The loco was being wheeled at the time. The leading boxes duly entered the horns, and so did the drivers. Confident that the trailers would do the same, the chargeman lifter, old Peter, didn't even look at the trailers, but just said to his crane drivers, "Righto, lower away," and they did. But the trailing boxes had not entered, and as the loco was lowered down, the new liners that had been put on in the fitting shop, were just peeled off like a machine slicing bacon! Luckily no one was hurt. Of course, the trailers had to come out again, boxes stripped off, and a second dose of machine and fitting shops before they could be reassembled and the engine wheeling completed. Needless to say old Peter was more careful next time!

About the most obstinate job I came across, during my stay, was on a "I3" tank, No. 91. My mate Bill, and myself, had her for quite a light repair job; but part of it included getting the cross-heads off the piston rods. All the motion work came down O.K., so did the connecting rods. A wedge was then placed between the special "removal" gudgeon pin, which we inserted, and a "button", (short piece of hardened and tempered steel), which was popped inside the crosshead's hollow neck, and thus pushed on the end of the piston rod. It was then a case of hitting *upwards* with a sledgehammer, which we swung between our legs.

Bill had a go, I had a go, time and time again; and after about an hour we got the first one off. In spite of trying everything we knew, the other one wouldn't budge! Next day we tried again. Still no joy. Bill reported it to "Peaky" who

57

said, "That's easy, we'll get old Jack up on it." Mad Jack came up, and spent the morning on it, even bringing up his 28 lb. sledge, which was known as a "Monday hammer", but still it refused to budge. Mr. Worsley, the foreman, was told; and he fetched in turn, every fitter who was known to be good with a hammer, from other gangs, to try their luck. Word spread round the whole works, and anybody in the end was welcome to come and have a go! Still the same result. It was next arranged for the Boiler Shop to send an oxy-acetylene welder round to heat up the crosshead to expand it, before hitting it. Another day was spent with this set-up, but all in vain. Mr. Worsley then decided that it must come off, so ordered the complete cylinder block to be removed from the frames. This took Bill and me several days, as the bolts had to be drilled out. However, the cylinder block was at last removed, and taken out and stood in the centre road. Now the hammer could be swung as the navvies used to, breaking up the road, vertically *downwards*.

Mad Jack was procured once more, with his "Monday", and the whole shop stopped work to watch. After about a dozen really heavy blows there was a report like a field gun being fired, and the crosshead was off. A cheer went up from all the fitters, and it was all over. Both crossheads were then loaded into a truck and sent to Ashford Works, where they had special gear for plating the tapers inside the boss, which in effect built up the taper so it didn't go on quite so far.

Like all the other apprentices, I eventually got put on a Stroudley "D1" 0-4-2 tank for general repair. All these Stroudley tanks were still fitted with condensing gear inside their side tanks, which supplied the crosshead pumps. The exhaust steam was led back to the tanks by large copper pipes, and condensed back into water. It also brought quite a bit of cylinder oil over with it, so that the whole inside of the tank was covered in thick black oil!

A special oilskin was kept in the stores for this job, complete with "sou'wester"; I duly donned this outfit, and dropped into the tank via the manhole. There were several pipes to disconnect, including a swivel pipe like a tuning fork, which rose and fell from its small end on a float. Like this, it always collected water from about two inches below the surface, where it was hottest.

Well, I duly disconnected all the pipes, and passed them up to my mate outside. Then I was able to extricate myself and a fine state I was in! My mate and I then went outside, where there was a hose in the yard. Then I had to stand still, whilst he hosed me down to get rid of the oil. The oilskins having been cleaned were then returned to stores. After this the tanks themselves were removed, and sent round to the boiler shop.

Refitting all the gear was never so bad, as a lot of the oil had been removed at the tank overhaul in the boiler shop. Even so it was not a pleasant job. When all was complete "Peaky" was informed, and he booked the tanks in. The apprentice then got extra pay in his packet for this job called "dirty money".

Bill and I were working on a D3 class "Bogie tank", and the boilermakers were required to get inside the boiler to examine it. We removed the top half of the dome, which exposed the regulator. Now the boilermakers reckoned that they could not get into the boiler, via the dome, whilst the regulator was in place, so the fitters had first to go in and remove the regulator, to allow them to enter!

I was assigned the task of removing the regulator, and was about the largest of the boys in our gang. The widest part of me got stuck as I was going in, and Bill did no more than climb up and stood on my shoulders and *pushed* me in!

Once inside, I found that I completely blocked the available space, and couldn't even reach the nuts that held it in, let alone release them. After a lot of advice from Bill, as to how I could do it, he finally decided that I was too big for the space, as I had been telling him!

Then came the job of getting me out! Every time I exerted any strength my muscles expanded, and I got stuck. Bill tried to pull me out, but he couldn't. In the finish he got hold of the crane, and passed a rope around me under the armpits, and the crane driver very gingerly lifted me out!

Then Bill "borrowed" the smallest boy in the shop, one named "Eric", and even he could only just get in, and work in that confined space.

Once the regulator was removed, of course, everything was plain sailing. Even the boilermakers were able to get in! I learned that this particular class was very bad for this job. The dome aperture was much smaller than on most of the other classes.

About this time, the Works Fire Brigade were short of volunteers, and a notice was posted up on the shop notice-board appealing for recruits.

"Mad Jack" decided that he would join, and was duly accepted. His training included the celebrated "fireman's carry", in which an unconscious person is carried out of a burning building, over the fireman's shoulder.

I have already told how Jack's new mate, James, was not very strong, and one day Jack was working in his usual fashion, and it proved too much for James. He fainted, and went down on the floor like a dead man!

Jack didn't hesitate. He grabbed his ankles, and slung him over his shoulder, then ran down the centre of the shop with James, hanging head down, and his arms hanging straight down, on his back.

A cheer went up from someone, and it was taken up by others, as Jack made his way down to the First Aid Room. By the time he reached the door at the end of the shop, which someone was already holding open for him, the whole shop was cheering!

Jack returned to us a few minutes later, to explain to us what had happened; but it was quite some time before James was sent back for return to duty, none the worse for his "fireman's carry".

Soon after this Bill Ramsey (of bucket fame in the Brass shop) was involved in an escapade that might have had very serious consequences, but luckily no-one was hurt, not even Bill.

I have already told how a gas pipe ran along in the pit, and we had flexible pipes coupled to any convenient tap below. The business end of the pipe carried a piece of flattened copper pipe, and this was useful not only for seeing with, but as a portable blow-lamp for warming up obstinate nuts.

Bill and his mate were stripping a smokebox, about a couple of engines down from me. They were so engrossed in their work, that they didn't notice the time, until the works hooter blew for the dinner hour. Bill's mate, not wanting to get down in the pit to turn off the gas, plunged the end of the pipe down into the heap of dirt and ash (which always abounded in smokeboxes!) and of course this extinguished the gas. He then came out and shut the smokebox door.

When the time came to resume, Bill got a whole page from a large newspaper, lit it in "Peaky's" forge, then got up on the runningplate with it. The smokebox of course was now full of gas, and as soon as Bill opened the door, with his fiery torch in his hand, there was a report like a naval gun firing!

The force of the explosion blew the door wide open, and snapped the safety chain which limited its travel, so that the door hit the outside of the smokebox with a crash. This in turn dislodged all the loose soot inside the box, and when we came running up to see what was to do, all that was visible was a huge black cloud of soot, through which we could just see the grinning face of Bill Ramsey!

He was luckily on the engine side of the door at the time of ignition, so the door was blown away from him, and was luckily on the side to escape the blast. Otherwise he would have been blown off the runningplate, or knocked off by the door, and would most certainly have sustained some injuries.

On yet another occasion, we had just taken the coupled wheels out of a "Mogul", and as soon as the engine was up, clear of the wheels, they began to run down the shop, because of the very large balance weights on this class. Bill Ramsey said, "Just look at those wheels running away."

My mate, Bill, said: "Put yer foot under 'em, that'll stop 'em." Bill Ramsey went to do just that, and would have done so, had it not been for one of the other fitters, who lunged into him with his shoulder, and knocked him down on the floor!

The wheels carried on down the shop, until they crashed into several more pairs taken from other engines, sending up a cloud of sparks, and lifting them bodily off the floor with the impact.

The last locomotive built at Brighton for the L.B.&S.C.R. 4-6-4T "Remembrance" ready for the dedication ceremony of March 1923 outside the General Offices in the South yard.

ontal view of the loco. The "Iron Man" building of the boiler op in right background. Buffer heads, lamp brackets, door ages etc., have been "whitewashed" for photographic purposes.

Lt. Col. Lawson B. Billinton C.B.E. Locomotive Engineer at Brighton Works 1912–1923. He retired upon formation of the Southern Railway Co. in 1923 and engaged in fruit farming near Bolney.

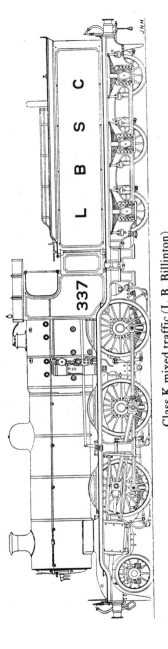

Class K mixed traffic (L.B. Billinton)

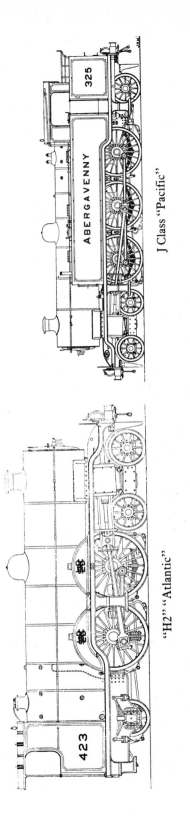

J Class "Pacific"

"H2" "Atlantic"

D.E. MARSH EXPRESS LOCOS

62

Chapter Six

Trial Trip

My friend Henry Parrott had managed to get out on a trial trip, and suggested that I should try and do the same. I mentioned this to "Peaky", and he was agreeable, and told me to write a letter to the Works Manager for permission. This I did, and handed it to "Peaky", who gave it his blessing and took it in to the office.

In due course, the request was granted; and "Peaky" was told to choose a suitable engine. We had an "N" class "Mogul" in the gang, No. 863, and it was arranged that I would go trial on her.

The trial driver, at this time, one named Freddie Queen, a quiet, congenial soul, was going over the engine out in the yard, when I approached and told him I was going with him on this trip. He examined my footplate pass, and pronounced it in order.

By the time Fred had enough steam and was ready to go, the morning was well advanced. We left the yard, and were given a path to Eastbourne, not very far in advance of the Eastbourne portion of the "Sunny South Express", which left Brighton about mid-day.

Fred did not want to hold this up, so he let 863 go over the viaduct, and had worked up to about 60 between Moulscombe and Falmer; quite a bat for a loco of this type on trial! There was a good deal of noise in the cab, and it seemed to me as if the end roofing sheet was loose, and banging about.

Fred said this class always did that at speed, and was what the drivers called "the big end hitting the roof". He was not at all happy with her however, and came to a stand outside Falmer signal box, although he had the road. He asked the signalman to let him go back in the loop beside the platform, and as soon as we were safely off the main line, we jumped down to inspect.

The "Sunny South" went sailing by as we did so, and Fred said they should never have sent him off so close in front of it.

He could smell something hot he said, and made his way to the left-hand cylinder. The piston-rod was right out at end of stroke, and it was a beautiful shade of blue! "Packing too tight," said Fred. As it was a special type of metallic packing, it could not be eased out like the old asbestos type. He went back up into the cab, and returned a few minutes later with some green worsted trimmings, and a tin of what he called "Tecalpot". This was a very thick black

63

cylinder oil, so thick that when cold you could invert the tin and it would stay put. As the tin had been up against the boiler backhead, this lot was warm and fluid!

He made up a sort of horseshoe of worsted, and soaked it in the oil, then put it on the end of the packing gland like a swab. As soon as it touched the rod, the oil started to spit and boil, just like cold fat in a hot frypan! It went up in smoke, and Fred kept pouring more oil on to it. Having got his swab where he wanted it, and used half his tin of "Tecalpot", he had a quick look round at everything else, which luckily was O.K.

He went down and had a word with the signalman, and got a clear path for Lewes, with nothing behind him this time! He decided to take it easy to Lewes, and there have another look at it. If it was no better, he would go no further, but take her back to Brighton.

I could see visions of my trial trip ending prematurely!

Off we went, steadily, to Lewes. This gave me a chance to have a go with the shovel, and I managed to get nearly as much coal over the floor as in the firebox. At Lewes, we got in the sidings again, to have another look at the rod. I was very relieved to see that its colour had now returned to normal! Fred examined it, and gave it some more "Tecalpot" on the swab. He decided it would be O.K. to continue, so off we went to Eastbourne, to the running sheds there.

Upon arrival, we had another look at it, and it was quite O.K. Fred didn't even bother with any more oil! He decided it was now time for us to eat. After our sandwiches, and flask of tea, Fred and I went all over the loco, even getting down in the pit to inspect underneath.

He found one or two small items not to his liking, and I adjusted several things until he was satisfied. We then proceeded to the turntable, and turned her round for the return journey. The tender tank was replenished at the water crane, and then off we went.

We were getting alone fine, until just after Lewes Station we were brought to a dead stand by an adverse signal; just short of the tunnel under the road there.

I asked Fred if I could take the regulator when we got the road, and he agreed. As the signal came off, I eased the regulator up a bit. Nothing happened! So I gave it a bit more. Still nothing happened! I then opened up a bit more, and Fred, seeing how much I'd opened up, rushed over and closed it. I soon found out why. The old girl had started to slip furiously! We moved forward slowly into the tunnel, and filled it with steam. We couldn't see anything ahead for steam! The effects then began to wear off, and Fred gingerly opened her up a bit and got us out of the tunnel.

I didn't do any more "driving" that day! He explained to me that with a superheated engine, it was necessary to open up slowly, and then "wait for it" as the headers and elements had to fill up to boiler pressure before she'd move.

Anyway he took her along in great style, and drove her back into the yard outside the works.

I went and saw "Peaky", and had to relay my day's experiences to him. Old Fred came up later and told "Peaky" that the engine was now O.K. and he was going to report it fit for traffic duties.

I was the last apprentice to go for a trial trip on the footplate!

Henry was also responsible for a second trip I made, unofficially, some years later! During the early 1930's, as the main lines were being electrified, the authorities decided to acquire a "Sentinel" Railcar for operating the branch which ran up to the Devils Dyke. Upon delivery, this car had to do a certain mileage before it could be handed over to public service, and quite a few troubles befell it, and it made many visits to the works for sundry adjustments.

After one such visit, Henry had inquired of the driver if it were possible to have a ride on it to the Dyke and back. He was told that if he liked to get over to the shed one day just before it left, and get aboard without being seen, he, the driver, would have no objection. Henry mentioned this to me and suggested that I should go along with him for moral support.

It was duly agreed between us, so one fine day we both managed to slip away without being seen, and crossed the main lines to the shed. We found the railcar in the yard, and Henry had a few words with the driver, who told him the departure time. We were told to join it just as he was about to start, and keep out of sight! This we did, and off we went!

This was very different from my first trial run. Here was no noise or vibration at all. Just the clicking of the wheels over the rail joints, no exhaust beat to speak of, just a purr of the multi-cylinder engine. I believe it was a single acting multi, very similar to the one used on the firm's steam road lorry, and was supplied by a vertical, high pressure boiler. It made heavy going of the climb up to the dyke, and upon arrival the driver left his cab and proceeded to the other end to the controls in a second cab at that end.

Henry and I had got out on the platform for a stretch and nearly got left behind, as the driver was off again in a few moments. We should have been stranded up at that lonely outpost for heaven knows how long, as it was only making infrequent runs, at no set times.

However, we did manage to get back on board and the trip back was much quicker as it was all downgrade. Upon approaching the works and yard, we were told to keep out of sight once more, and to leave it, on shed, without being seen. We thanked the driver and departed. No one ever said anything about it, so I suppose we weren't spotted. We arrived back in the works, having been missing for about a couple of hours, but we apparently hadn't been missed, and no one even asked where we'd been.

There was quite a bit of trouble with the brakes on this car. It had large cast iron drums bolted on outside the wheels, with large air cooling holes in their sides. The shoes were lined with linings similar to car brakes of the period.

Sentinel's men came down to modify these brakes in the works and I got talking to them. They told me that the fault was really with the Southern's operating department. The car was supplied with a choice of three gear ratios, and the request was for the *highest* of the three, to give a top speed of nearly 60 m.p.h. on the level as they didn't want it to delay the newly-introduced electric service between Brighton Central and Aldrington Halt, where the Dyke branch left the main line.

The makers had advised the *lowest* set of gears in view of the heavy climb from Aldrington to the Dyke, but the company would have the highest. Consequently the car frequently stalled on the grade and had to stand still for a "blow up". Worse still, on the descent, there was not so much retarding effect from the engine on the higher gear, so the brakes had to do all the work. They got very hot in the process and the car had been known to sail straight through Aldrington Halt non-stop and only succeeded in stopping at Hove with the greatest difficulty!

Wider drums and brake shoes were fitted, and this did help a lot, but it was usually touch and go coming down, if there was much of a load on.

The car did eventually go into service, but did not last very long. It was not designed to take a trailer at busy times, so could not satisfy the traffic demands. It was eventually transferred to the Westerham branch in Kent, and the radial 0-6-2 tanks with one or two coaches reinstated.

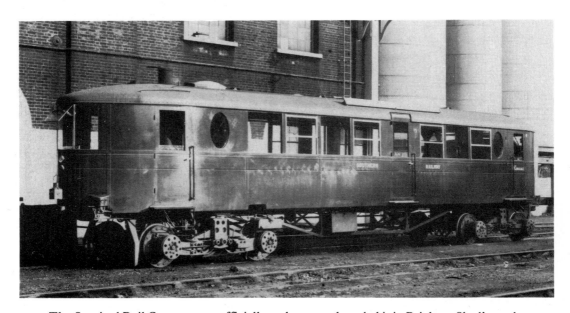

The Sentinel Rail Car as we, unofficially and unseen, boarded it in Brighton Shed's yard.

66

The pedestrian entrance to the South yard from platform 9 of Central Station. A watchmans box controlled the entrance, and the watchman is outside having just received a package from the bowler hatted foreman on the "Terrier" tank engine. Circa 1908.

Baltic Tank No. 328 majestically brings the "Southern Belle" into Brighton Central and is just passing the Boiler Shop. Circa 1922.

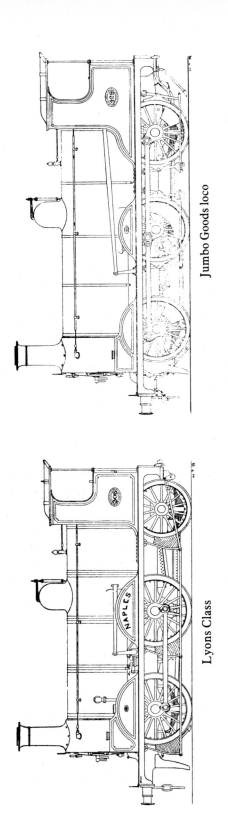

Jumbo Goods loco

Lyons Class

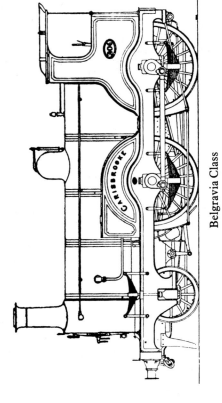

Belgravia Class

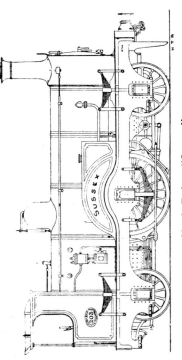

Single Driver "Sussex"

STROUDLEY TYPES

68

Chapter Seven
The Fitting Shop

Before leaving the Erecting Shop, mention should be made of a very successful rebuild of Marsh's "I1" class of 4-4-2T.

As built, these were very indifferent machines and enjoyed but a poor reputation. The whole class of nineteen locos were rebuilt at Brighton between 1925 and 1932. The rebuild included new cylinders, and a larger boiler; the latter became available as the larger I3 class received superheated boilers, their existing saturated boilers were given to the I1 in the rebuild. I did not work on these myself, as they were done by Charlie Wright's gang on the other side of the West bay to me, but I followed their progress with keen interest.

The rebuild transformed these machines. They were very lively, and could accelerate rapidly. They became prime favourites with the men, instead of being despised by them!

All good things come to an end, and so my happy days in the Erecting Shop had to end also.

I was instructed to report to Mr. Pilbeam, foreman of the Fitting Shop, one Thursday morning, and had another change of number, and back on the Machine Shop clocking-on racks.

I was sent to work with old Charlie Burgess, whose gang had been so depleted under the "running down" policy that he was the only one left! His only job was eccentric straps, fitting new white metal liners into the straps, then sending them round to the machine shop for turning. The old chap was very quiet, not saying much to me or anyone else, but every now and then looking all around the shop, over the top of his steel framed spectacles.

After my exciting life of the last few months, I found this boring in the extreme! Only one uninteresting job in the whole gang, and running the jobs to and from the machine shop on a sack truck!

However, it was not to last long. Charlie only had about a month to go before he retired, and as all his orders had now been completed, the job came to an end, much to my relief.

I was then sent to work with another "one man band", named Ted Allsop. He was a real "live wire", and was doing all sorts of little "odds and ends". He also ran quite a profitable side line in the shape of a sweets and tobacco shop, in his cupboard under the bench!

He could pull his face into all sorts of fantastic shapes, and often made us laugh, by being able to persuade his top plate of false teeth to advance forward from his mouth, until they were about half-way out. He would have done very well on the Hippodrome everybody agreed.

We were not very busy, and the time was liable to drag quite a bit. I took advantage of the slackness by making myself a few tools, such as callipers, tap wrenches, and scrapers. I also served in the shop quite a bit when Ted was absent!

The only gang that was remotely approaching busy was Bill Williams', across the gangway. Bill had a big store and tool cupboard, like a double wardrobe; and on the inside of both doors were the very latest in "pin-ups" of the period.

By modern standards, they were quite tame, but they gave the boys a thrill in those days! On one occasion the Works Manager, Mr. Hackett, came up about some job or other. Bill went to the cupboard to get something out, and Mr. H. caught sight of the pin-ups.

"Shut the doors, Williams," he said. "It's disgusting. They're not fit for any decent man to see." Old Bill shut the doors, and then taking his pipe out of his mouth, said dryly: "Well, there's no decent men up here Sir!" Mr. H. did not go much on that last remark, and as soon as he had finished his inspection, he beat a hasty retreat back to his office. Anyway the pin-ups stayed till the end of the gang!

The end was not long in coming. One morning Ted had a letter from the office saying that it was regretted that his services would no longer be required, after the end of the week. He had been expecting it for some time, and had a sweets and tobacco shop with his wife in the town, so was not unduly worried. He shook hands all round during his last week, doing no work at all, and I was only working for myself. On his last day he gave me a few small tools, as he said he didn't think he'd ever get the chance to use them again at his age!

There were three other gangs in the shop; one run by Bert Watts, which did expansion links and all the motion work generally; one under a chap named Glendinning, which was disbanded soon after I started in the shop, before I had much chance to find out what they did!

The third was run by Jimmy Pratt, a very humourous, dry, little chap, who, whatever part he had finished, would smear oil all over it, to stop it going rusty! When I asked him why he was smearing an all *brass* component with oil, he retorted, "I oil up *everything*. Can't be wrong then, can you?"

Jim did a variety of jobs, but mostly connecting and coupling rods in my time, as nearly all his other work had gone.

The above three chargemen, and Bill Williams, I never had the chance to serve under. Glendinning vanished and was probably made redundant. Bill Williams I believe, on reaching the age limit, retired. This left Bert Watts and Jimmy Pratt.

They, and the few youngsters that made up their gangs, were transferred to the south end of the Erecting Shop, East Bay. They had a bench each, just inside the big doors; and between them they did all the work previously done in the entire fitting shop. They were both still there when I left, and Bert Watts at least continued right through the war years, and up to the British Rail era.

The old Fitting Shop was then closed. It had been a total loss as far as I was concerned. I learnt less there than in any other shop, as it was too late, all the work had gone. It came as a great relief to me, when the office boy came up to me on a Wednesday afternoon with a letter.

I was to report to Mr. Bates on the Thursday morning, and transfer to his department – the millwrights. Once more, I was the last apprentice in the fitting shop!

The millwrights were still in the bottom of the fitting shop, in fact they were the only people left in it. At least they had plenty to do, because, apart from keeping everything in repair, they were getting up machinery and loading it into trucks for Eastleigh and Ashford Works.

We will have a new chapter to deal with my experiences with them.

Works manager Joe Ellis, in bowler hat at left, was always present to see the 8.03 a.m., which 4-6-4T No. 328 is just starting, leave for Victoria. The date is 1919 and fireman Osborne leans from the cab to say "Good morning".

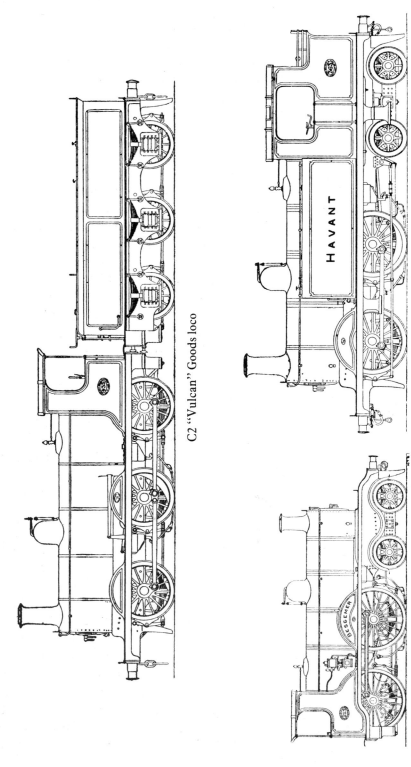

C2 "Vulcan" Goods loco

D3 Bogie Tank

HAVANT

B2 "Grasshopper" Express

R.J. BILLINTON TYPES

Chapter Eight
The Millwrights

I reported to Mr. Bates, a very tall man, even without his bowler hat! I learned later, that he was a crack shot with a rifle. He was a member of the Southern's rifle team from Brighton and used to go to Bisley with them.

He in turn, told me to report to chargeman Charlie Green, a short, dark, wiry man, with, at times, quite a quick temper. He was always all right to me however, although he did have several occasions to "tick me off".

In this gang, each fitter had his regular labourer, and Charlie moved me about to work with each one in turn. There were only two besides himself. Harry Beale, approaching middle age, who worked mainly on the bench, repairing lathes, mills, drilling machines, etc. Quite a nice chap; I didn't have very long with him as the management transferred him to Eastleigh Works. The second chap, Tom Fry, had not long to go to retirement and was very short winded! Many times, in coming to work he had to stop to have a "blow up" as the others put it; in other words, stop for breath.

I worked quite a bit with him, and as one of the others put it, "You won't break anything with him." He was very careful and slow!

Then there was Charlie himself. I spent more time with him than anyone else. We would have one, two or three labourers with us, as the job required. In charge of the labourers (self appointed) as one of them described it to me, was one named George Sandifer ("Sandy", of course!)

"Sandy" had been a Chief P.O. in the Navy, and had been in the Battle of Jutland. He would do all the rigging up for lifting or moving anything, and would swing about up in the roof trusses like a monkey!

This was remarkable really, as I learned that most of his inside had been removed, and he was equipped with man-made tubes. He must have been very tough, as it didn't seem to make much difference to him. He was a glutton for work, and I got on very well with him. From him, I learned how to place slings on machines to lift them without damage, and how to shift heavy machines with jacks, and on rollers. Little did I realize then, that this knowledge was going to stand me in good stead in a few years time when the second world war burst upon us. The factory where I was had a lot of equipment sent in by the Ministry of Supply. I had to take charge of the unloading and installing of the various machines, as I was the only one who'd had any experience in this sphere! I often thought of old "Sandy" when I was sitting on steel girders in the "black-out" unloading machinery by moonlight!

However, to return to Brighton, the others in the gang were Bill Denny, Charlie Green's own personal assistant, who had changed his name from "Welfare" by deed poll. Quite a beefy chap, and very good at all the labouring and "slinging" that Charlie required, although no match for "Sandy" with ropes and tackles.

Then we had Bill Trussler, a quiet chap, very nice too. He travelled to and fro with me to work and home, as we both got out at the same station, Shoreham-by-Sea.

The last man, Tom Ridge, was quite a character. He had been in the Great War, and had seen service near some Italian divisions, "Wops," as he called them. "Dirty b——s they were too," said Tom. Always laughing and joking, and never downhearted, he was always the life and soul of the party. When anyone had any comment to pass on time booked on a job, Tom would always come up with his saying, "You don't get much engineering done for a shilling!" Of medium height, and very wiry, Tom would tackle anything, and was "Sandy's" favourite to help him, when he was fixing tackle, etc. up in the roof.

There was another senior fitter in the gang, named George Long. Soon after I joined the gang, George was solely engaged on testing and examining the cranes and all the lifting gear, ropes, slips, chains and chain lifting blocks. He had a labourer always with him named Horace Field, another jolly smallish character, who had been labourer in Arthur Peake's gang, in my Erecting shop days.

George also was a nice chap, although inclined to be moody at times. He was a first class fitter, with a wide experience of all millwright's work.

My friend, Henry Parrott, and another chap not long out of his time named Ford, were also in the gang when I first joined it. The last named was not at all popular, and I don't think many tears were shed when he was declared redundant!

Henry worked mostly with George Long, who at that time was busy on machine repairs, and removing them for loading to Eastleigh and Ashford Works.

Sandy was in charge of the other "slingers", Tom and Bill, and was engaged in getting the machines up off their sites, and getting them into the Erecting Shop. There the crane would pick them up, and load them into the open 10-ton trucks, pushed into the top of the Erecting shop's east bay for the purpose.

Charlie drafted me along with them, to do any skilled work they might require, e.g. take off any overhanging parts, so that they might not get broken. The slingers were not allowed to use spanners, files, hammers etc., under Union rules, that's what I was there for!

I was also allowed to help supply the brawn required in lifting and shifting the

74

machines. Once Sandy had the machine in the truck, then it was secured with ropes, and then sheeted up with a tarpaulin. All this was new to me, but I was a willing pupil, and I've already told how it came in jolly useful later on.

Well, we eventually had removed all the machines that Ashford and Eastleigh wanted, and were left with a motley collection, mostly of old obsolete machines. The "Selection Committee" from the two Works came and had a last look round, to see that nothing useful had been left. They found one or two, and duly marked them with their initial, either "E" or "A". The rest were just classed as scrap.

After we had loaded the last of the "wanted" machines, I was told to retain Tom and Bill, and break the rest up for scrap. Three heaps were to be made. Non-ferrous – (bronze bearings, wheels, etc.); mild steel – the shafts, nuts and bolts, handles etc.; and cast iron – the bases, pulleys etc.

No time limit was fixed on the job, so I dismantled everything in the proper manner; i.e. as if I was going to replace it after it had been overhauled. This gave me quite a lot of useful knowledge that would also come in useful in the war to come, when I was engaged on repairing machines that I had earlier installed.

Anything that did not respond to the above treatment, my two mates were allowed to smash out with sledge hammers!

This occupied the three of us for a considerable time, as counter-shafts and the line shafting had to be dismantled as well. A glance at the illustrations of the Machine Shop will show how extensive this was! When we had enough in our three scrap heaps, this also had to be wheeled into the Erecting shop next door, and loaded up.

When we had completed this macabre task, I had to inform Mr. Worsley, who by now was in charge of machine fitting and millwrights departments, as well as his Erecting shop. The shop was then declared empty and closed, thus saving rates.

We next turned our attention to a boiler house, underneath the main south yard, on the way down the slope to the iron foundry. Here were three stationary steam boilers, which had supplied steam to the steam hammers, and for works heating, in the happier days, now alas, gone by. "Sandy" was again sent to take charge of this, and the drill here was to "borrow" a pukka boiler wagon from the Boiler shop, which of course, ran on the standard railway track. We, therefore, had to build our own trackbed, lay our own rails, then get the boilers on to the wagon and with crowbars under the wheels, propel them out into the yard, and along to the Goods yard crane. This was able to lift them, swing them out over the wall, down into a "main line" boiler wagon, waiting in the Goods yard below. Sandy secured them on to this with the chains provided, and away they went. Two went away, I know not where. The third was taken up in a goods train to Lover's Walk yard, transferred to the main line, then backed into the station, then into our South yard. Here we rescued it, and installed it once more in the old

Smith shop, where it was used to supply the solitary steam hammer that had been retained for the only two blacksmiths remaining.

Both were nigh on retiring age. One was Bill Coop, an old Swindon man. The other was Ernie Munro. I believe he had once been at Derby. Each had his own forge. One each side of the steam hammer.

I remember that quite a big job (for these times) was required, and Bill had one piece in his forge, and Ernie the other half. Both halves had to be brought up to welding heat, then united under the hammer.

Bill wanted to do it his way, and Ernie of course, his way!

By the time they had finished arguing, the job had cooled down too much and was no good! Mr. Worsley came round, now also in charge of the smithy, and settled it by saying, "Coop will be in charge. The job will be done his way."

The next time the job came out O.K. Soon after this old Ernie retired, so no more arguments ensued.

From time to time the gland on the hammer needed tightening, to stop the steam leakage. Old Bill would spot me walking down the shop, and call me over.

"How'd you like the first house at the Hippodrome tonight?" he'd ask with a twinkle in his eye. I knew what he meant, and said I would like it. "Right," he'd say, "I'll see the boss, and tell him this gland needs pulling up."

Bill always would have this done during the dinner hour, so as not to hold him up. This meant that my day finished at 4.30 p.m. instead of 5.30 p.m., as in my days with Ted Smith in the Brass shop. I can't say that I ever used that hour to go to the Hippodrome though!

Also in this shop was a huge metal shearing machine, mainly for cutting the long lengths of steel bar used in the machine shop. The machine could be started up, and would take quite a time to reach operating speed. Then, the horizontal jaws would open and close slowly but surely. A piece of 3-inch diameter steel bar could be dropped between them when they were fully open. They would close as if nothing was there! The machine just gave a shudder, and a grunt, and the piece of bar would fall down, just as you would slice an apple with a knife!

To enable it to do this, it had a flywheel weighing 4½ tons mounted in a pit below it, and connected to the shears by gearing; it was duly commandeered by Eastleigh, and Sandy was given the job of removal and loading, with me to do the dismantling.

We had a truck in the bottom of the shop, and the Smith shop travelling crane overhead, which was rated at 8 tons.

Well, everything went all right with this, as the largest piece the crane could manage. The fun came when Sandy shifted the flywheel! He looped a single wire rope sling round the rim and slung it up on the crane.

George Slaugher, the crane driver, took it right up as high as he could get it, then came down the shop with it at his maximum speed! This crane was about the fastest in the Works, and I had to run to keep up with it. Sandy followed behind at his usual pace, his running days being long since past!

Tom Ridge was standing in the truck, waiting to receive it, and I was to help guide it into place when we reached the truck. We had gone over half way, when through the "wicket door" in the end of the shop came Mr. Worsley, accompanied by the Works Manager, Mr. Hackett.

The latter looked at the flywheel in horror, "STOP! STOP! Lower it down!" he cried. George did as he was told, and Sandy caught up with us.

"Fancy hanging that great wheel up on the crane with that bit of string," said Mr. H. "You might have killed somebody."

"That's not string," said Sandy. "It's a six ton wire rope!"

Mr. H. looked aghast! "All right," he said, "but next time use a chain, it *looks* better." This quite upset old Sandy. He kept repeating it for the rest of the day.

The sequel to this was that George Long was instructed to gather up all wire rope slings, and withdraw them from service. This went all right until he came to Sandy, and asked for his. "You're not having mine," says Sandy. "Mr. H's orders," George repeated. "Tell him to go to hell!" says Sandy. "Bit of string be b——!" "O.K.," said George. "You know the orders. If you want to use them, you do so at your own risk. I've warned you."

And Sandy carried on using them. Although Mr. H. later saw him doing so, he never said any more! He probably realized that Sandy had not cared about the German Navy at Jutland, and certainly wouldn't care about him! Even if he sacked him, there was now no one else to take his place, the nearest substitute would probably have been Tom Ridge.

The next thing to claim my attention was the pulverised coal plant at Eastbourne Running Shed. Engine No. A629, one of the Maunsell "U" class Moguls, had been converted in 1930 to burn pulverised coal.

For this, a special plant had been erected at her home shed, by the boiler-makers at Brighton, and a great friend of mine in later years, who now alas is no longer with us, helped to erect it. His name was "Bat" Collins, of blessed memory.

The experiment was not a success. I don't think the loco was really of a suitable type for this type of firing, as its firebox was too short. The flame used to hit the front of the box, and swirl back round the sides, playing on the trailing axle-boxes, which were repeatedly running hot. She was converted back to standard, and we had to go to Eastbourne every day from Brighton, to dismantle the plant. No one was sorry about this. All on the loco, driver, fireman, and any of the loco testing department staff on her used to get filthy. They nicknamed her "the dust cart!"

Tom Fry was given the job, and Sandy sent along for the lifting. I was also attached to the party mainly, I found out later, to do most of the skilled work, whilst Tom went out into the surrounding fields to collect watercress from the numerous streams, or "dicks" as he called them, which abounded in the very rural surroundings of this particular running shed!

We had to book on earlier than usual, to catch the 7.30 a.m. out of Brighton station, and we had to leave Eastbourne in the mid-afternoon to arrive back in the Works before it closed at 5.30 p.m., so the job was rather long drawn out.

Neither Tom nor Sandy liked this job very much, as it was right out in the wilds. I remember one lunch-time, that a "Vulcan" 0-6-0 Goods engine was being turned on the turntable, with a good old "sou-wester" blowing.

We were having our usual stroll round after our meal, and we were passing nearby. The fireman called out to us, to go and lend a hand to get her round. He explained to me that, as she came round into the wind, it would catch her, and he'd be unable to hold her, and drop the stop catch in as well. Some crews had been round two or three times under these conditions before they could stop their loco!

We duly finished our dismantling, loaded it all into trucks and sent it to the scrap merchants. All were relieved when we were able to resume normal working hours back at Brighton.

The works shunter, originally No. 82 "Boxhill", is restored to original condition and "Stroudley" livery. Taken in Brighton locomotive yard 13-4-58. The three tanks in the background belong to the water softening plant.

The morning exodus for London: Outside the North end of Brighton Shed "L" Class "Baltic" Tank No. 328, ready for the 8.05 a.m. to Victoria: "J" Class "Pacific" tank No. 325 ex Abergavenny ready for the 8.15 a.m. to London Bridge. "L" Class "Baltic" tank No. 333 "Remembrance" ready for the 8.45 a.m. to London Bridge, "The City Limited". The loco. works in the left background. The date is the summer of 1925.

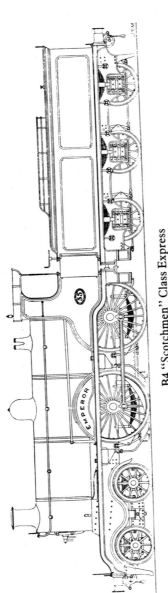

B4 "Scotchmen" Class Express
R.J. Billinton

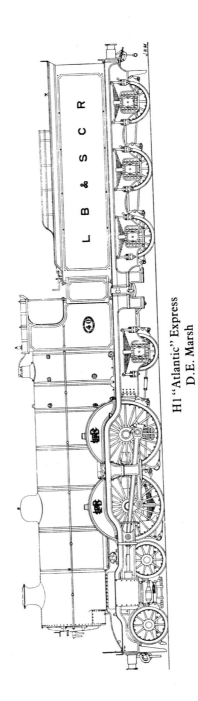

H1 "Atlantic" Express
D.E. Marsh

80

Chapter Nine
The Erecting Shop Once More

On the 27 October, 1933, a letter from the office was handed to me stating that my apprenticeship was completed, and I had the chance to stay on as a temporary fitter until the end of the year. Of course, I accepted, and was put back in the erecting shop, in the gang of "Dan Hastings", a very tall, thin man, who spoke with a slow country drawl, and who had two enormous feet, which, when he walked, took up the position known as "twenty to twelve".

A very mild and kindly man, Dan teamed me up with another young chap, like myself, just out of his time, and named George Ellis; who later on, after the war, became Works Manager!

Also in the gang was one old fitter, near retiring age, named Bill King. Now George and I, being young and eager, started on any engine given us, stripped it down in double quick time, and whilst waiting for the materials to come back from the various shops, would start another engine to save hanging about.

In the meantime, the materials for the first one would come back, and Bill King and his mate would then go on, and build the engine up. As he was much slower than George and I, he had a lot more time booked on the engine than we did, and when the piecework balance was worked out, he had a better balance than us, because of his greater number of hours on the job.

Secondly, we were stripping, and working in all the dirt, whereas Bill was building and working with clean repaired parts, so didn't get anything like so dirty as we did. Old Dan soon noticed this, and mentioned it to us, saying that he didn't like us working harder on the dirty jobs, and getting paid less! Well, George decided that sooner or later we would have a chance to get "even", and we'd carry on as we were. The chance came much sooner than I had expected.

Dan had given us a S.E.C.R. "Wainwright" 4-4-0 and we were stripping out the smokebox, about the dirtiest job you could imagine! The week was drawing to a close when we started, and George was determined to finish this job by the Friday afternoon, as he did not want to go back in there on the Monday morning, when we would both have clean overalls on.

Our engine was sited just to the north side of the "Crossing", on which Mr.

Worsley, the foreman, always used to stand about 5.0 p.m. on a Friday, talking to his second-in-command about the week's progress.

The crane drivers packed up lifting about the same time, as they had to clean and oil up the cranes for the weekend.

Bill King, several engines down the line, had already stopped work, and had washed his hands, ready for 5.30 p.m. finish. He was standing warming his back at our gang's fire. We had managed to get everything out except the chimney liner, which was a big heavy one on this class. It had been freed of its bolts some time earlier, and George had decided some time previously, that we would wait for the conditions outlined above when we couldn't have the crane, then shout out to Bill King for assistance.

As soon as Mr. Worsley was settled on the crossing, I got out on the front runningplate just above the buffers, and bawled out at the top of my strong voice, "Bill, come up and give us a hand with this chimney liner." Bill looked aghast. He looked at me, and could see Mr. Worsley looking straight at him! He had no option but to come on up to us.

"Whatd'yer want?" said Bill. We explained the situation to him of how we wanted this liner out by 5.30 p.m. but couldn't get the crane. Reluctantly he climbed up on the footplate, and Mr. Worsley was smiling to himself, as he knew what was about to happen.

The plan had been worked out in great detail beforehand. I, being the largest and strongest, would go right inside, up the back end. We would lift, turn the liner 45 degrees to let the lugs come through the hole in the smokebox; then lower. I was to pull it towards me, causing it to tip sharply above Bill King, opposite me. Everything went fine! I tipped it more than I expected and a great shower of loose dry soot, which had been resting on top of the lugs, cascaded down, all over Bill King!

He looked like one of the minstrels in the "Black and White Minstrel Show". Even Mr. Worsley made a joking remark about his plight. Poor old Bill! It was now nearing 5.30 p.m. and he hadn't been so dirty in years! George and I of course, were full of apologies, and helped dust him off with a broom!

Old Dan thoroughly enjoyed it, and told us afterwards how pleased he was to see old Bill do a dirty job for a change!

After this Dan was able to arrange things a bit better, so that George and I stayed on our own engine all the time, and we got more reward for our labours. At the same time, Bill had to do his own stripping.

About this time I teamed up with my friend Henry Parrott, and we took an H1 Atlantic No. 37 for a "light repair", mainly "wheels and axleboxes". Having removed these, we were told to strip the smokebox, as the boilermakers were coming on after that was completed, to remove the flue tubes from the boiler. Whilst engaged on this, I noticed to my horror that there was a large crack running from one tube hole to its next door neighbour. Henry examined it and confirmed my discovery. We fetched old Dan up to see it, and he in his turn reported it to Mr. Worsley. The latter informed the Boiler Shop, who then decided that we should remove the boiler entirely from the loco, and send it into the boiler shop for a new tube plate to be fitted. This we duly accomplished, so we finished up with an "H1" stripped down to its bare frames, with just its cylinders and valves left in position, which made it virtually a "general repair"; quite a feat for two "journeymen" to tackle on their own, being one of our largest class of tender locos.

Just above the crossing where the smokebox episode took place was a doorway, leading into the machine shop. It was like an oversize domestic door frame, made of wood, but carried no door. The engine I was working on was on the south side of this door frame, and the engine on the north side of it was being repaired by another young journeyman named Reg Cooper.

Reg was a very athletic type and a wonderful swimmer and diver. He was rather hung up for materials, so hadn't much to do; arriving at my loco, he stopped for a chat, saying how bored he had been all morning with nothing to do. He decided he'd liven things up a bit after the lunch break!

Upon his return he had acquired an ordinary reel of black cotton, as used by gardeners to place over the top of new sown grass seed to deter sparrows! Reg drove a small nail into each side of the wooden frame, and stretched a piece of the cotton between them, across the frame. He then retired under his engine to watch the fun, and I found a job in the cab of my engine, that I might also enjoy it.

The first chap through the door was rather tall, and walked straight through it, breaking it with his chest without even knowing it. Nothing daunted, Reg tried again, and it was very amusing to watch the antics of the various men as they touched the cotton. Of course, if broke straight away, so they couldn't see anything, even if they did stop to examine the site.

Meanwhile, Reg had shifted camp up into the cab of his engine, as he had a very hearty laugh, and didn't want to give the game away! I think I laughed as much at the laugh Reg gave, as I did at the poor victims!

The climax came in the middle of the afternoon, when a middle-aged man from the boiler shop, rather short of stature, came on the scene. Reg had got the cotton just at the right height for him, and he caught it just under his nose!

He reeled back like a drunken man and then, recovering, came forward again, with his arms flailing in all directions, seeking the obstruction. Of course, he had broken it, so found nothing! He looked all round the place without success, so gingerly resumed his journey.

As soon as Reg had recovered sufficiently from his fit of laughing, he nipped down into the doorway, and replaced the cotton. Hardly had he got back in the cab, when I espied our friend heading back on his return journey. He had evidently forgotten his previous encounter, as he walked straight into it once more!

The result was just the same as before, except that when he reeled back, he trod on the toes of another man following close behind him, and a fine old argument ensued!

The boilermaker insisted that something had caught his nose. The other chap said he must be barmy (or words to that effect), as there was no one else near. Certain that something fishy was taking place, the boilermaker, who must have been very short sighted, then carried out a minute inspection of both sides of the door frame, at a range of about one inch; but he still didn't see Reg's tacks and broken cotton!

In the meantime, Reg could hardly control himself, and was just about doubled up with laughter. I myself could not work for laughing, and my sides fairly ached by the end of the afternoon.

I was glad when 5.30 p.m. came to put an end to it, as I hadn't felt so bad through laughing during the whole of my eight years at the works as I did that afternoon!

Soon after this Dan Hastings acquired an "H2" Atlantic No. 421 booked for several jobs, one of which was loose cylinder retaining bolts.

Our driller, one Fred Mepham by name, another tall thin man like Dan, but with normal feet this time came on, and drilled out the bolts which had to be replaced. The holes were cleaned out with a "rose bit" to the next size larger. Machine shop then supplied new bolts, which were supposed to be a driving fit.

Somebody must have slipped up on the size of these, as they wanted an awful lot of punching in, but Dan said he didn't mind, as he wanted them tight. They got worse; and finally, the last one to go in on the first cylinder got to within about 1½ inches and refused to budge.

Dan examined it through his glasses. "Ought to go," he said. "Can't see anything wrong with it. Fetch me our 'Monday hammer'." He piled into it for all he was worth with this 28-pounder, but it didn't go in very far. He couldn't keep this up very long, as he ran out of breath. Small wonder, because he was near retiring age! I had a go, and George Ellis had a go, and slowly but surely the bolt was going home.

But it got tighter still! Dan was determined not to be beaten, and in the finish, only he and I could deliver a blow strong enough to move it, George held the punch for us, and Dan and I supplied the brawn. We won in the finish, but it had taken the best part of the morning for three of us to put one bolt in! After this, Dan reported it to the machine shop foreman, and had the size reduced slightly. The second side went in very much better than the first.

Early in the 1930's the Southern's C.M.E. Dept. produced the "Schools"

The Bulleid "Pacifics" have recently been credited with introducing the 4-6-2 wheel arrangement to the Southern Railway constituent companies. Here we see the Brighton's first "Pacific", brand new in 1910, being propelled in the loco. yard by a "Terrier" tank engine over 30 years before the first "Merchant Navy". The chimney of the works Boiler House is visible above the "Terrier's" cab.

The L.S.W.R. also had 5 similar though smaller locos. in 1922.

4-6-4T No. 329 "Stephenson" backing out of Brighton loco. yard to take charge of the "UP" "Southern Belle" express. A "B2X" 4-4-0 in background. September 1922.

R. J. Billinton Class "C2" 0-6-0 Goods loco. No. 521 over the Inspection Pit by the "West" signal box in Brighton shed's yard. A 4-6-4 Baltic Tank in the background. Circa 1922.

An R. J. Billinton Class "B4" 4-4-0 No. 59 on Brighton shed circa 1920. The only Brighton loco. to have a single upswept curve to the running plate. This it acquired in 1912, together with a "Phoenix" superheater. Upon the latter's removal in 1915, the curved running plate was retained. Sister loco. No. 70 "Holyrood" made the fastest ever time from London to Brighton with steam power in 48 mins 41 secs in 1903. 90 m.p.h. was attained near Wivelsfield.

class, one of the most capable and excellent locos ever to run in this country. Originally built to work on the restricted clearances of the London–Hastings service, they eventually saw service all over the system, and inevitably some found their way into Brighton Works.

We had quite a few engines sent in about this time for "light repairs", mostly "wheels and boxes", and Dan was given one of the first "Schools" into Brighton, for wheels and boxes. George and I started on this one, and the drill was first to remove all the spring hanger bolts between the springs and the "J" hangers running underneath. We could then remove the springs, whereupon the cranes would take the loco into the centre road, where stays would be removed; thus the wheels would be freed.

On the large "Brighton" classes built in this fashion, i.e. all the "modern" types, the spring hanger bolts had quite a "coarse" thread, i.e. not many threads per inch, and the nuts moved fairly easily. Not so on the "Schools"! Here we had very fine threads, i.e. a large number per inch, and the nuts wouldn't budge.

George was in the pit, heating them up with the gas, and hitting the sides with his hammer, whilst I, outside on the level tried, with a large spanner, a long piece of tube on that, and a large crowbar in that to undo them. We did manage to move all the driving wheel ones, but not very much, then they locked up solid!

The trailers, around the hot ashpan, and with water from the various overflow pipes in the cab going over them, never even looked like moving!

Our foreman, Mr. Worsley, had been watching us with interest, and could see that we were in great difficulty. A 'phone call to Eastleigh Works confirmed that they were immovable, and that they cut the bolts in two with oxy-acetylene cutters, and fitted new ones on assembly. So a new set of bolts was sent along to us from Eastleigh Works, and our boilermakers came round with their cutter and made short work of the bolts! We had no more trouble after this, all the rest being quite straightforward.

In S.E.C.R. days the C.M.E. Dept. at Ashford had designed the ill-fated "K" or "River" class tanks. These were very good locos on the road, as regards performance and haulage, but their riding qualities left a lot to be desired. These were built at Brighton to the same design as the original No. 790 of 1917.

They could (and did!) roll alarmingly! After several minor mishaps, the lay press referred to them as "The Rolling Rivers". This culminated in the nasty accident near Sevenoaks, already referred to, when No. A800 "River Cray" came right off the road as she was passing under a bridge, and the coaches got smashed against it, killing thirteen people and injuring dozens.

The whole class was immediately withdrawn from traffic, pending the findings of the official inquiry, and they never ran again as tank engines. Their tanks and bunkers were removed and stored at Ashford, together with their rear bogies, and they reappeared as tender engines, to do good work. Even so, some drivers still said that they had a tendency to roll.

I suppose the sight of all those tanks, bunkers and bogies, lying idle in Ashford Works Yard, was too much for the "powers that be", and the outcome of it was the "W" class of the early 1930's: 2-6-4 tanks using up the aforementioned parts.

These locos were barred from passenger trains, after the previous unfortunate experience of this type on this duty; and worked freight trains *only*, mainly at night.

They were three-cylinder jobs, and as one was departing from Haywards Heath early one morning the whole of the inside valve motion collapsed, and got mixed up with the track! After the wreckage had been cleared to enable it to move, it was towed to Brighton Works and examined.

The experts decided that the brackets holding the expansion links were not strong enough, so they were sent back to Ashford Works (the brackets that is), where gussets were welded in to fill up the open sides.

Dan had been given this job also, and George and I did it. A "U" shaped stretcher ran across the frames between the tanks, and the brackets were bolted to this.

Owing to the very restricted working space, the bolts had to be removed by wedges and packing, the holes opened out to the next size larger, and stronger bolts inserted. This was so successful, that it was decided to do the whole class, without waiting for any more to collapse!

George and I did the lot, one at a time of course, but it was quite an awkward job, as only the bare minimum of parts was removed from the centre of the engine, and boiler and tanks remained in position.

The Southern was always ready to try out new ideas, and in 1934, No. 1850, an Ashford "N" class Mogul, was fitted with Marshall's valve gear. So that it could be tested against a standard engine of the same class, it was required to be fitted up with the pipes and controls to take indicator diagrams. It came to Brighton Works for this, and Dan was given the job.

Dan, George and I studied the drawings on the bench. We all agreed that a lot of it was impossible, and would need to be modified. For instance, the drawing called for a ¾″ gas tapping hole in each end of the cylinder, on a vertical axis. Owing to the low cylinder location on this class, we found that no drilling appliance we had at the works could be brought to bear, because they were all too long to get in there.

We told Dan this, so over to the Drawing Office he went with the drawings. "What's the matter? Don't you know how to make a ¾″ gas tapping hole?" asked the draughtsman.

"Course I do," says Dan, "only it can't be done in the position you want, unless we get both cranes and hang the engine up in the air whilst we drill them all!" "Well put 'em where you *can* drill 'em, and we'll alter the pipes to suit,"

The western facade of the works and entrance to the loco. yard as seen from Platforms 2 and 3 of Central Station.

The only "Atlantic" to carry a name in L.B.S.C.R. days, No. 39 "La France" so named to haul the train carrying the French President M. Raymond Poincaré from Portsmouth to London in 1913. On shed at Brighton in the early 1920's.

The prototype of the author's "Gladstone" 5″ gauge model No. 200, ex "Beresford"; on Battersea shed in 1924.

The last locomotive designed by W. Stroudley and completed by R.J. Billinton in 1891. No. 158 "West Brighton". It spent the last 7 years of its life (apart from a few months at Eastbourne shed) on coal stage piloting at Brighton. It was withdrawn in September 1934 in truly shocking condition! Ex L.S.W.R. stock on West Coast line in background.

said the draughtsman. This was duly accomplished. But similar snags arose; as the engine was complete, something or other was in the way! Dan spent a lot of his time running over the Drawing Office about this, and they got a bit nasty about it. So did Dan!

"It's all right for you b——s," said Dan. "If there's anything in your way you can get a rubber and rub it out, but I *can't*!"

"Look Dan," says Chief Draughtsman, "you know what we want you to fix up?"

"Course I do. I've done it many times before," says Dan.

"Right. Go back and fix it up in your own way when you can't do it to drawing. Let me know when you've done, and we'll come over and make a new drawing to suit the job you've done," said the Chief Draughtsman.

And so it was! We fixed it up to Dan's specification, and they duly came and made their new drawings. They also complimented old Dan on making a first class job of it.

This, of course, is by no means the first instance of the shops doing the job, and having drawings made to suit; but it was my first experience of it!

Interior of the cab of a Brighton "K" class "Mogul" 2-6-0 locomotive. This class survived "en bloc" until the end of steam power at the close of 1962.

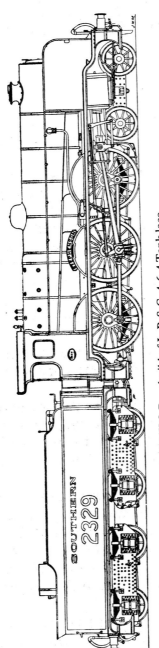

N15X S.R. rebuild of L.B.S.C. 4-6-4 Tank loco.

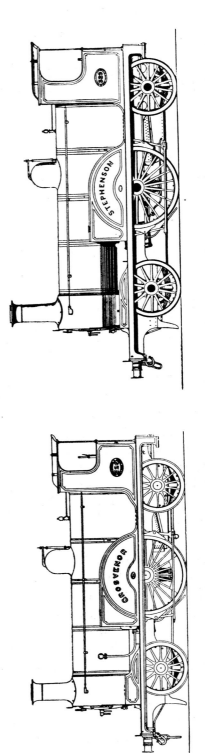

STROUDLEY SINGLE DRIVERS

Chapter Ten
Back with the Millwrights

My joy at being back in the Erecting Shop was not to last for very long. Work was getting shorter and shorter, and the erecting shop was taking in more and more carriage work, and less locomotives.

Being one of the very few men now left in the works who had any experience of millwrights work, the management decided that I would be best employed there from now on.

This proved to be my last move, and I was to finish my days with the Southern Railway Company in the company of Charlie Green and his merry men.

Brighton Works had its own water supply drawn from its own well about 120 feet deep. Two sets of triple stand pipe pumps (one in use and one stand-by) were located in an "engine room" below floor level in the north end of the old smith's shop and immediately above the bore hole proper. Long rods, supported by wooden guide blocks fastened to the well sides, led the drive downwards from the three throw crankshafts to the actual pumps, which were located in the "wet headings", about 112 feet down. A vertical steel ladder, attached to the side of the well, gave access to the headings.

Charlie Green was the only skilled man in the works who had maintained this gear, and I was instructed by Mr. Worsley to find out all I could about the pumps and well, as he realised that the said Charlie would not last for ever! As it turned out, he was still there when I left to take up a job with Brighton Corporation Waterworks.

However, it was not always possible to get down to the pumps for servicing, as in a wet year the water level would not go down low enough to uncover them. Any time after about early May, the level would uncover them, until somewhere about October, in a normal year's rainfall; and all "wet heading" work would have to be done then. All the hours booked at the bottom of the well also carried "danger money" with them, and this of course enhanced the ordinary "day work" rate, which was all you got in the Millwrights.

On my first descent, Charlie gathered his labourer Bill Denny, and myself together, and produced his list of the tools and gear required. Bill stowed all this into three sacks, one each, and off we set for the engine room! "We mustn't forget anything," said Charlie, "as it's a long way to come up from the bottom to fetch it."

He led the way, Bill after him, and I brought up the rear. It was an uncanny experience! It was pitch dark going down that vertical ladder. We stepped off the ladder on to the heading staging at the bottom into light! Marine type bulkhead lights were installed at the bottom, and Charlie had switched them on in the engine room prior to getting on the ladder.

As soon as we had recovered out breath, Charlie ordered the sacks to be unloaded: "To see if we have forgotten anything." Everything checked out O.K. to my relief, when Charlie suddenly turned to his mate and exclaimed, "Gor blimey Bill, we've forgotten the chalk." Both looked at each other aghast! Then, turning to me, he said, "Slip up and fetch it Bert, will you? It's on the bench, in the engine room."

But I had been there long enough to take my bearings, and realised that here, at the bottom, there was no brick lining! All around us was pure, virgin, Sussex chalk; hundreds of tons of it!

I reached out and took a piece off the heading's face, nearly as big as my fist, and handed it to Charlie.

"Will this do until we go back up again?" I asked. He looked at Bill and the pair of them burst out laughing. "Yes, you've rumbled it," said Charlie. "We always try this out on everyone who comes down for the first time, and you'd be surprised how many have gone back up the top for it," he chuckled!

No joke, climbing 112 feet of vertical ladder to fetch a piece of chalk!

After this we settled down to dismantling the set of pumps not in service. New seatings and valves were fitted, but the water had not gone low enough for us to get to the foot valves, so we had to leave these. Charlie said he'd do them when he got a year dry enough to lower the level enough, but hadn't had one for some years.

We then changed the sets over, and dealt with the other lot, so both sets were overhauled, in case they could not be done again, maybe for two or three years.

Whilst down below, I was taken on a tour of the galleries or "headings" and shown the spot where the original prospectors had to hurriedly "down tools" and run for it, as the water came gushing up. The tools were alleged to be still down there; the water had never fallen low enough since then to uncover them!

Some years previously, Mr. Bates, the last foreman of millwrights when employed as an ordinary fitter, had swum around the headings! Someone wagered that no one would be able to do this, as the water was quite cold! Bates took him on, removed all his clothes, and dived naked into the water. He swam all round the headings, then returned to collect his wager!

The water was on tap through an ordinary bibcock in the smith's shop, above a huge trough that the smiths used for quenching their red hot lumps of iron.

All visitors to the Works were told to try our water. It was wonderfully cool even on the hottest summer day.

There was a huge water main, carrying it across to the tanks mounted up in the air, over the running sheds and outside the Works. These tanks were coupled up to the various water cranes, and the locomotives took their supplies from them. Brighton water was voted by the drivers to be the best on the railway: it had no additives in those days, being pure spring water!

I have already mentioned how, in the contraction of the works, the "machine shop", such as it was, was now located in the south end of the west bay of the Erecting shop.

Just inside the door was a wheel lathe for all the wheel turning jobs, operated by a character known as George Thursby. He was as bald as a badger, and was always chewing tobacco!

Next to him was Harry Howes, working a "brass finishing lathe". He did any small brass fittings, including re-boring valve bodies and making new rams to suit, for the numerous hydraulic jacks sent in by all the running sheds for repairs.

The repair of these was my exclusive province during my second stay in the millwrights.

Opposite to these two was a horizontal boring machine, worked by one "Gunner Jones", another tobacco chewing addict! And next to him was a small drilling machine, taking up to ½" drills, driven from the line shafting overhead through a "fast and loose pulley", on the machine itself.

Charlie Green called this a "sensitive drilling machine" and the "loose" pulley of it gave him a great deal of trouble. It was very little used, so the driving belt spent most of its time on the "loose" pulley which, being of small diameter, ran round very fast. This caused the bronze bush inside it to wear out frequently, in spite of Charlie fixing a grease cup to it, and making sure it had plenty of grease fed into it.

The machine was used by anyone needing to drill a small hole, no regular operator being assigned to it. Larger holes were attended to on a small "radial" drill, also operated by "Gunner Jones".

Now the flat belt for operating the "sensitive" passed from the countershaft, round two idler pulleys at the back of the "head" and then round the pulley at the top of the spindle at the front of the machine. This pulley was hollow, and placed at a height of just about level with the average person's forehead.

A favourite trick of "The Gunner" was to fill this pulley with "suds", a mixture of cutting oil and water, which looked just like milk! As soon as anyone started the machine this suds mixture would fly out of the pulley, into the unfortunate operator's face!

Charlie Green had inspected the "loose" pulley only a short while before, and found it worn out once again. He had told me that he was going to try to get permission from Mr. Worsley to replace the bronze bush with a ballrace, and had departed to the office to put his plan to Mr. W.

I was busy changing the grinding wheels on the "Lumsden" grinder on the other side of the shop, when Charlie appeared accompanied by Mr. W. They went straight to the "sensitive", whose pulley, unbeknown to either, had previously been "loaded" by "The Gunner", who also was unaware of their intended visit. In fact, none of us knew of it, or it would have been "unloaded"!

Everyone carried on with their work as if nothing was amiss, praying that no one would start up the drill. Charlie was standing alongside the loose pulley and Mr. W. in the operator's place facing that pulley! Both were rather short of stature fortunately!

To prove his point, Charlie threw the striking gear over, starting the machine. Instantly, Mr. W. took two rapid paces backwards having caught the full force of the revolving suds with his bowler hat! He removed the hat and proceeded to shake it to remove the last of the suds! At the same time, he was looking all round him, to see if anyone was laughing, as if so, there was the culprit!

Luckily, everyone kept a straight face and carried on with their work, denying all knowledge of the incident. The outcome of it was that Charlie was allowed to fit his ballrace, which proved to be a great success. Mr. W. gave the machine a wide berth in the future, and "The Gunner" gave up his pulley loading antics for a considerable time!

Brighton's second "Pacific" turned out by L.B. Billinton in 1912 and named "Bessborough". This was the first of eight Brighton locos. to have Walschaerts valve gear, here shown in close up. It has been stated recently that these 8 locos. had "outside admission" valves, most likely because the return crank "trailed" the crankpin instead of leading it. But the rocking levers fitted inside the frames reversed the motion of the top ends of the combination levers so that the "inside admission" valves moved normally.

Whilst it was L.B.S.C. property, and for the first ten months of its life, "Remembrance" ran nameless in a "primer" coat of red oxide with just its number on the bunker. Seen here on Brighton shed's turntable in 1922. Regular driver Harry Funnell by rear buffer.

Three months after acquiring Southern Railway ownership the name had been painted on the tanks and the livery changed to "Dove Grey" lined out in black and white; this was purely for photographic purposes. However, it had now covered enough mileage to be near its first general repair. After this had been accomplished it was repainted in the light green at first used by the S.R. and returned to traffic in May 1924. Seen here on Brighton Shed in 1925.

The authors splendid engineering miniature "Remembrance" face on view.

Chapter Eleven

Epilogue

Several changes in the day to day life in the Works took place during my stay. The most important of those was undoubtedly the abolition of the ban on smoking at work.

During my first two years, it was strictly prohibited whilst at work, and rigidly enforced, most probably because of the fire risk; but with the increasing use of the oxy-acetylene torch and its attendant shower of red hot sparks, it made it seem rather ridiculous.

Human nature being what it is, men would have their smoke anyway! Some would smoke in difficult to observe locations, such as fireboxes, bunkers, smokeboxes, and even tanks! The air was likely quickly to become foul in these circumstances. By far the most popular "smoking lounge" was the lavatory! Men would go "down below for a coupla drags". This also meant a look at the paper, so the men would be missing for at least 15 minutes.

The management realised this, and it was considered worth trying the experiment of smoking at work. I was in the Erecting shop at the time, working with Bill, in Arthur Peake's gang. It was amazing to me how few men took advantage of the concession at first. Most still "went down below"! Gradually, however, they came round to it; and then no notice was taken of it, men just smoking when and where they fancied. It was not all that enjoyable though, as with the inevitable oily fingers, oil penetrated the cigarette paper, and made the tobacco taste most unpleasant!

Much more useful to me, and also the rest of the train travelling staff, was the concession to use the Works entry and exit at the end of the Number 10 platform of Brighton Central Station.

At first, we had to walk right round the goods yard, through the back streets, then enter by the New England Road gate.

About the same time as the smoking concession, those travelling to work by train were allowed to use the entrance at the south-west corner of the bottom yard. We were able to catch a later train in the morning, and still clock in on time. It made half an hour difference, and was very acceptable, particularly in

99

the winter. We could also catch an earlier train home, so we gained both ends.

Another change concerned the method of paying "bonus" in the Erecting shop. At first, piecework rate of time and a quarter was paid every week. Every six engines completed, and a "tally" was taken. Any extra that the engine had earned, was paid out as "balance", and good paying engines would make this quite a sum (for those days). Some wouldn't reach the money paid every week, and these were "in debt". As the "good" paid for the "bad", there was usually something to come, however small.

However, with the decline in the volume of work, it became increasingly difficult to make the jobs pay their way, and most gangs got further and further into debt.

It was then decided, that, as the debts could never be redeemed, (the lack of work saw to that!) they would be written off. Daywork rate would be paid every week, and each engine assessed as before. If any balance was earned it would be paid; but if it didn't reach the daywork level, it would be abandoned.

Like this, it was impossible to get into debt, but you got any balance you were able to earn.

The old messroom at the bottom of the steps in New England Street was one of the first of the Works buildings to be taken for other purposes. It became a warehouse for "Fyffes Bananas".

A new messroom was opened, just above the old wheel shop, but it never became popular like the old one. Most men taking their midday meal with them, preferred to eat it in the Works, and make their own tea in a quart can on any convenient gas point.

It was strictly against the rules to do this, however, and every so often, a check up would be made.

Then the men would still eat in the Works, but they had to do it "on the run" from shop to shop, so as not to be caught.

There was never an official "tea break" either morning or afternoon, during my stay. Most men had it though, "unofficially".

The iron foundry was closed down, complete with its ball, which dropped from a great height on to old castings, to break them up into suitably sized pieces to put back into the furnace. It was never to re-open.

The same happened to the old Coppersmiths shop, which was situated outside the gate to the North yard, over the New England Road bridge.

All the rest of the Works was re-opened during World War II, and the plan of the Works, made in British Rail days, was substantially the same, except for the coppersmiths and iron foundry mentioned above. I am indebted to British Rail for permission to publish this plan of the Works as it was in World War II.

My happy days at the Works were fast drawing to a close. We had all been told to take any alternative job which came along, as our future employment with the

Southern Railway was very precarious. At last my chance came! Having answered an advertisement in the local paper for a job with Brighton Corporation Waterworks, I was called for interview, and accepted. Then it was my turn to hand in my notice to the office, instead of the other way round.

I was one of the very, very few to do this, in those days of depression before World War II.

I was not to stay long with my new employers however. Within five months I had entered the motor trade.

After a few weeks with these people, I was asked to go into partnership with an old colleague in the motor-cycle trade. This was to prove ill-fated within two and a half years, but I stayed in the motor-cycle trade until World War II inevitably claimed me in the country's drive for arms.

I found myself back in a factory's maintenance department, and was soon unloading and installing machinery.

That, however, is another story, and has no place within the covers of this book.

Brighton Works, of course, was reborn, and very busy on armaments and locomotive construction. I could have returned, and as I've already told, was even asked to go back. I decided against it, however, and probably just as well. After the war was over, the same old thing happened again. The Works was run down once more. It eventually closed, and is now mostly demolished.

The fine locomotives turned out in turn for the L.B.&S.C.R., the Southern Railway, and lastly British Railways, are now, alas, all broken up, except for a few preserved examples.

Up till the outbreak of war, my leisure, and indeed, all my time, had been taken up with racing and servicing motorcycles. Hitler caused this to terminate in September 1939, and my adventures in the realm of motorcycles have been set down in my work, "A Clubman at Brooklands".

My life was completely altered. I now worked at Langley, Bucks, and married shortly after. There was not much leisure time during the war years anyway. We were all too busy making munitions, but I could not settle down to inactivity during meagre leisure periods.

I secretly yearned to be back amongst my beloved steam locomotives, and decided to construct one of my own, and as already recorded it's parentage was a product of Brighton Works!

A serial had appeared in the "Model Engineer" in 1935 and 36 describing the construction of a Great Northern Atlantic in 3½" gauge. The Brighton version was almost a replica, and as I already knew the variations, I made the necessary modifications to the drawings and got busy.

The location of the copies of the magazine proved quite a problem, and the acquisition of the necessary castings even more so. A near neighbour on my new housing estate had acquired a new "Gamage's" lathe just before war broke out. Luckily for me he had no idea of how to use it, and said I could have it for what he had paid for it.

It was soon installed in my spare bedroom, a new electric motor acquired, and the machine shop was ready! The "Brighton Works Annexe" was now in business, but as no castings had as yet materialised, a start was made on the boiler.

Some years later, a correspondent to the "Model Engineer" to which I was now a regular subscriber, described the most essential faculty required to produce a successful miniature locomotive, as the "Determination to overcome difficulties".

I found this to be very true, but with my old headmaster's pet saying "Nil desperandum" ringing in my ears, the "Atlantic" materialised to be operational in 1947. With the help of my dear friend Jack Austen-Walton, the loco. and tender were emblazoned with the Marsh "umber" livery, and sent to the "Model Engineer" exhibition in London in 1949 to be awarded the "A.J. Reeves" prize; awarded for the best loco. failing to qualify for a medal. The only faults the judges could find were that the livery was incorrect, (it lacked the dark "edging" around the panels) and that the chimney was incorrect. The latter was a Great Northern one, the only one available at the time, and when I look at the photograph of that loco. now I realise how horrible that chimney looked.

Some years later it annoyed me so much, that I turned up a new one from the solid, to exact dimensions taken from the works drawings, and this greatly enhanced it's appearance.

During some haulage trials conducted at Hove in 1950 it proved capable of hauling a load of ¾ of a ton, whilst in 1954 it made the best performance in the 3½" gauge class of the locomotive trials conducted by the Sussex Miniature Locomotive Society (of which I was one of the founder members) at Haywards Heath. It repeated this in 1955, again taking the class award and hauling a load equal to 1150 tons at a speed of over 100 miles an hour, if the figures were converted to the equivalent in full size. I was very well satisfied with my first attempt at locomotive manufacture!

As soon as the "Atlantic" was completed, and fired with the success it had achieved I decided to become more ambitious, and to go in for an even larger 5" gauge loco. Now back in my native Sussex, I made contact with a fellow ex-apprentice Jack Fuller, who by now had risen to the post of foreman of the Erecting shop in Brighton Works. I wished to make a replica of "Remembrance" the last loco. built at Brighton for the old L.B.&S.C.R.

Jack arranged with the management for me to have the loan of some fifty drawings, of the general arrangement and details of the famous "L" class Baltic Tanks. Not content with this he managed to acquire two pieces of steel plate

One of Marsh's inglorious "I1" class 4-4-2 tank engines at rest on Battersea Shed, just before Grouping of 1923. These locos. were reputed to be the worst steamers on the line!

An "H2" "Atlantic" on New Cross Gate Shed in 1926. No. 422 was the first locomotive's cab entered by the author, upon his appointment to the Erecting Shop.

In 1927 Stroudley's famous "Gladstone" was withdrawn, purchased by the Stephenson Locomotive Society and sent to York Railway Museum, after having its original livery restored.

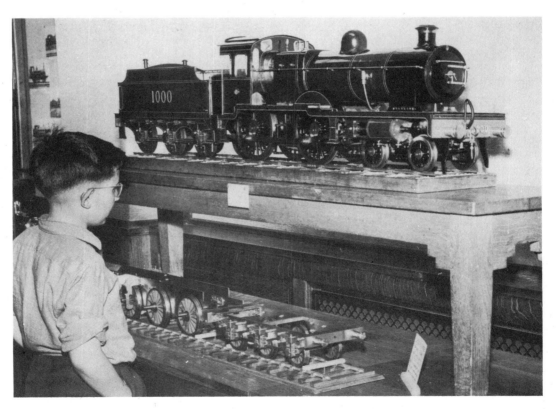

The 5″ gauge 4-4-0, based on the preserved Midland Railway No. 1000, loaned to Worthing Museum for their exhibition of railway items in the mid 1960's.

$^3/_{16}$" thick, of a suitable length and width to comprise the main frame plates. Few miniature loco's could claim that their foundations came from their sire's birthplace, but this one had such an auspicious start!

A toolmaker friend of mine, the late A. V. Hebblethwaite agreed to make me the patterns, and an excellent job he made of them all, leaving only the cylinders to be dealt with at a later date. As in the case of the "Atlantic" a start was made on the boiler. This was completed and tested within nine months and put on one side. Castings had now materialised from the patterns and frames began to take shape, and the wheels were fitted in provisionally.

By now, I began to realise the magnitude of the task that I had undertaken. Not only manufacture was involved, but designing to the odd scale of $1^1/_{16}$" to one foot, and everything had to be custom built. Nothing could be obtained "off the shelf".

I dearly wanted a 5" gauge loco. of my own to run, as although the "Atlantic" was very good in it's class, it could not reproduce the thrill of being in charge of a 5" gauge loco. I also realised that the creation of my brain child was going to take considerably longer than I had anticipated. It had to be correct in all external detail, and worthy of the memorial to the L.B.&S.C.R. that I intended it to be.

Although the full size engine had been named "Remembrance" to perpetuate the memory of the fallen railway employees in the Great War, it also had a secondary duty to fulfil in commemorating the L.B.&S.C.R. itself; and it's name was changed from "Victorious" to "Remembrance" at the eleventh hour with this end in view. It was this secondary function of the loco. that I set out to fulfil, little realising at the time that in a few years, every Brighton express loco. except "Gladstone" in the museum's care, would have passed into oblivion.

I therefore decided that I must have a 5" gauge loco. to run, whilst 333 took shape, so I inserted an advert. in the "Wanted" columns of the "Model Engineer" for a chassis of the type being then currently described in their pages, which was a Southern Railway 4-4-0 "L1" classed called "Maid of Kent". I would make my own boiler. The outcome was the acquisition of an outside cylinder version from a builder at Bromsgrove, Worcs., who was building one he intended to resemble a Midland Compound loco. of the L.M.S., but a 2 cyl. Simple instead of a 3 cyl. Compound of the original.

The builder had started just about everything and made an excellent job of it all. Even the boiler was started, but to my dismay I found it would not fit in between the frames in spite of all my efforts to increase the lateral dimensions between frames. There was no other way than drastic surgery on the existing boiler, short of making a new one from scratch. I therefore amputated the lower part of the rear end of the firebox, and was then able to fit the boiler into the chassis. Having solved that problem a new one raised it's ugly head! Having now coupled up the piston rods to the crossheads, and the valve spindles to their rocking lever drives, valve setting commenced, and revealed serious errors in the valve events.

The late K. N. Harris, himself a valve gear expert, had recently retired to within a few miles of me, and I enlisted his aid. Even he was baffled by the readings we obtained, but after a lot of time had been wasted on various complicated remedies the culprit was eventually diagnosed. The reversing shaft was in the wrong place!

With this component restored to it's rightful habitat, the valve events, although not giving to my mind, an efficient steam distribution, at least indicated that they would enable the loco. to function.

And so it proved to be on the track. The loco. performed very much better than I anticipated in view of its valve events, and gave many years of excellent service. It proved capable of hauling a much heavier load that its size would suggest, after I had carried out several modifications to its weight distribution, and amazed several owners of much larger loco's with its performance.

Stove enamelled in the old "Midland Red" lined out with black and yellow, and an L.M.S. coat of arms on the cab side, it was a most handsome beast. The only thing to detract from its appearance was the cab, which had to be made to the Southern "L1" dimensions and was much too wide. I had hoped to have fitted a scale Midland cab but this would have given a gap between boiler and cab front of some ¾" with the existing boiler. As I was not prepared to scrap an otherwise perfectly good boiler, working at 100 lbs per sq. in., there was no alternative to the somewhat ugly cab.

Several years of intensive operation with its attendant maintenance, took their toll on 333's progress, and by the time manufacture restarted, the full size scene had changed considerably.

The writing was on the wall for steam! Luckily the preservation movement got under way but it was regrettably, just too late to save any of my beloved examples from Brighton.

Several "Terrier" tank engines had been saved, one even going overseas to Canada! Our local Bluebell railway rescued a solitary E4 0-6-2 tank engine, and restored its original "Birch Grove" name on top of supposedly Marsh "umber" livery, which was of too pale a shade. Still, it was better than nothing.

It now became very obvious that my model would have a very important role to fulfil in the future. It would be the only three dimensional example of Brighton's largest express class, and the decision was thus taken to emblazon it with the full CORRECT Livery of the L.B.&S.C.R. so that generations as yet unborn would be able to thrill to the sight of this, straight from the paint shop example, as I had done as a boy.

It seems unbelievable in the austere days of British Rail, that the "Brighton" gave their loco's several coats of varnish to achieve this end. "Remembrance"

The 5″ gauge "Gladstone" ready to start work on the Worthing Society's track at Field Place. The safety valve simmers gently.

The latest effort Gauge "1" "H2" "Atlantic" No. 424 under construction, boiler complete and tested.

John Appleton, "Gladstone's" regular driver, lighting up at Guildford in the International Miniature Locomotive Efficiency Competition 1978 (July). He covered the greatest distance of any competitor, to finish third, and make the only non-stop run in his class.

The author steams the American "Baldwin" 4-8-4's boiler for the first time at Field Place September 1980.

Rear end view of the 3½'' gauge "H2" in umber livery.

My first attempt at a miniature locomotive, 3½'' gauge "H2" "Atlantic" No. 422 of blessed memory
in the works.

itself of course was never turned out in "umber". When it was "Brighton" property it was turned out in "Red oxide" primer, as were all other members of the "L" class when new.

The authorities were unable to decide on a suitable name for it, so it ran in primer with just the number 333 on the bunker for the first ten months of its existence. It had already been Southern Railway property for three months before it was turned out in "dove grey" lined out in black and white, and named with dedication plaques attached; at a special ceremony carried out in Brighton Works yard in March 1923.

It was NOT so painted, as has been recorded by another well known writer, in grey livery "In view of the solemnity of the occasion", but purely for photographic purposes. A number of pre-grouping companies indulged in this practice at that time, for examples that were to be recorded in their official files. "Abergavenny" had been so treated in 1910. Upon re-entering service in this grey livery, it was half way to its first general repair, from which it emerged in May 1924 in the light green shade that the Southern Railway used at first.

The Brighton "Baltics" have been the subject of much controversy, possibly more than any other class of loco. Even today people are writing to the various railway periodicals telling of how they were converted to tender loco's because they rolled, and after the Sevenoaks accident of 1927 were withdrawn and so treated. This was the fate of the ex. S.E.&C.R. "K" class tanks named after "Rivers" in Southern England.

True, they were converted to tender loco's in the mid 1930's, but because no suitable work remained for them to do as Tank engines, owing to the electrification of the Brighton main lines to the South Coast.

The other favourite error is to continue to state that they were converted to WELL TANK engines! The original one No. 327 was rather unsteady at first, and after near disaster at Hassocks in 1914 was withdrawn for modification.

The height of the side tanks was reduced, except for the outside sheeting, to preserve their appearance. Even so each tank still held 450 gallons, the EXACT CAPACITY of the SMALL WELL TANK which had been added between the frames.

The point missed by the people quoting the "Well tank" theory is that the BULK of the water, 1350 gallons of it in fact, was carried in the BUNKER! The only means of the well tank water reaching the boiler was via the "Weir" pump. The injectors drew their water supply from the bunker which was coupled to the side tanks, and filled from them. [I feel this digression was necessary as it is essential that ACCURATE information is recorded for posterity, whilst people in possession of it are still around to record it!]

With the preservation movement rapidly gaining ground and interest in steam locomotives increasing, work restarted on the chassis. I had moved house three times since starting the project, and with the workshop now settled once more, and housing more ambitious equipment, the cylinders were next tackled. In conversation with that eminent Swindon exponent, Lionel Woodhead, I had discussed the failings of the full size loco.; we both agreed that the original valves were too small, and suffered from insufficient travel for the cylinder size they were required to supply. I decided to increase the size and travel of the valve, determined that the model should not be "hamstrung" at the front end like the prototype. 1 inch diameter and ¾" travel was the target, and K. N. Harris, agreeing with my remarks on the prototype, offered to redesign the valve gear to give these figures. This he did, and it meant a considerable increase in the length of the combination lever and drop arm. In turn, I had to redesign the top anchorage for the front of the upper slide bar, and the rocking lever had to be altered to go across the top of the bar.

Only a few weeks before the first steam trials commenced, K. N. Harris died. We lost a great Steam exponent in him, and he was looking forward to seeing the results of the modifications, in which he had shown such a keen interest.

Steam trials in 1973 revealed several minor "bugs" to eliminate. These were soon dealt with, and the true potential of the model was attained. All who tried it were most impressed with the tremendous power it developed. The boiler proved to be an excellent steamer, and the valve gear enabled it to be "notched up" into mid gear, once it was well on the move; a state of affairs quite impossible on the prototype. Tanks and bunker were then finished off and fittings such as mechanical lubricators, and Westinghouse brake pipes added.

To complete the project I had it professionally painted and lined, using car cellulose paint; it was completed just in time to appear at the "Model Engineer" exhibition in London for January 1975. Here it was greatly admired, and was awarded a Silver Medal and the Crebbin Memorial Cup; for the best entry in the Locomotive, General Engineering and Mechanically Propelled Road Vehicle Classes; a fitting finale for twelve years work spread over a period of some twenty-five years.

With Brighton Works now demolished, and but a memory, probably completely forgotten in days to come, I was really back to "square one"; having disposed of my Midland No. 1000 now that "Remembrance" was finished. If I used it, damage might be encountered, and impossible to rectify.

In view of the important historical aspect the model had now acquired, I decided, very reluctantly, not to steam it. It was a difficult loco. to service. The rear bogie had to be withdrawn to remove the grate and ashpan floor, and it was very long and heavy to handle.

Lionel Woodhead, the Swindon exponent, came up with the answer. He had just finished his lovely G.W.R. "Bulldog" named appropriately, "SWINDON", and we discussed what he should do next. He wanted a complete change as he had only ever built G.W.R. loco's. Everyone I suggested he turned down. At last he got it. "How about a 'Gladstone'?" he exclaimed! "No bogie to worry about, and a nice easy tender." We exchanged glances and he could see he had started me off once more. "I could join in and we could build it together" I exclaimed!

And so it was decided there and then. I managed to locate Stroudley's original General arrangement drawing, from his report to the Institute of Civil Engineers of March 1885. A set was photocopied for each one of us from these, and a start was made early in January 1975.

I cut out the frames and did most of the "heavy" work, whilst Lionel concentrated on the smaller sections. We had decided straight away to "Swindonise" the valve gear, and Lionel was in his element here, designing and making this entirely.

Friend Bob Youldon meanwhile, made some excellent wheel patterns, and these produced some nice clean wheel castings from a Chesterfield firm, the only castings used on the entire loco. Everything else was cut from the solid.

I roughed out and preliminary bored a very tough piece of bronze for the cylinder block and turned it over to Lionel to finish, as his lathe was more accurate than mine. Whilst he dealt with this and the wheels, I got going on my speciality – the boiler! Progress was rapid. It had to be! I just did not have another 25 years such as I had spent on "Remembrance", and I wanted a loco. to run!

We had to have many a conference on this job. Clearances around the slide bars and front axle were extremely tight. The tender also proved to be anything but easy. Lionel agreed in the finish that it had posed more problems than any other that he had built.

In spite of all this it was ready for steam trials in eighteen months. It went very well and was an excellent steamer. The only "bugs" appeared to be weight distribution, to secure adequate adhesion. I made several modifications here before the considerable power available could be even remotely used.

Whilst Lionel busied himself with the tender, I set about producing all the "Brighton" accessories; chimney, dome, safety valve case and lever, cab sides, buffers, couplings etc. etc. I selected the number 200, as that was the last "Gladstone" to retain a Stroudly copper topped chimney. It still retained it in S.R. days, certainly up till 1924, probably even later.

The livery chosen was the L. B. Billinton one with just L.B.S.C. on the tender, and company coat of arms on the driving wheel splashers. These were effectively created in oil paints by friend Maurice Joly, a fellow "Brighton" enthusiast.

Once again car cellulose was chosen, beautifully applied, this time from an aerosol spray can by John Appleton, who is also 200's regular driver now. I suffer from cramp after a very short spell at the regulator these days. The final result is an unusual and beautiful model set off by it's white cab roof contrasting with the deep brown of the livery. It has been out "visiting" other club's tracks more than all my other loco's put together, and is always greatly admired.

Wallie Coney, whose father was "Samuel Laing's" driver in full size, and had travelled many miles on a "Gladstone's" footplate, drove her around the Beech Hurst track and remarked that she rode and sounded exactly the same as the prototype. The beat is very soft, as the original was, she steams well and is extremely frugal in water and fuel consumption. She has the immeasurable advantage that the prototype lacked – a "radiant" type superheater and mechanical pump lubrication for cylinders and valves.

John persuaded me to enter her for the International Miniature Locomotive Efficiency Trials which were held at Guildford in July 1978. The fuel issued was a hard anthracite which normally requires a hard blast, the very thing she lacks!

As most people were having trouble with the fuel and getting short of steam, or having to shed some of their load as they could not climb the 1 in 80 bank, I instructed John not to worry about fuel consumption. He wanted to make a non-stop run, which no 5" gauge loco. had attained up till then.

In spite of being kept on the steaming bay for a good 10 minutes with a boxfull of lovely red hot fuel, (all booked against him) he climbed the bank in great style, being cautioned at the TOP of it, by the observer for being *above* the permitted speed! He went on to record the only non-stop run of the day in his class, and was loudly applauded at the finish. In the excitement a lot of fuel was spilled on the cab floor, some inevitably lost overboard, so in spite of having covered the greatest distance of any competitor (one and a half times that of the 2nd. man) the fuel booked against him relegated him to 3rd place. However, everyone agreed it was the best run of the day.

The figures (converted to full size equivalent) told that he hauled approx. 600 tons at a speed equivalent to 125 m.p.h. No. 200's designer the great William Stroudly, and regular driver Dick Harmon, would have been delighted if the full size loco. could have hauled half that load at 80 m.p.h.!

It was certainly a wonderful tonic for me and a tribute to "Brighton" works. It certainly behaved in true Brighton tradition!

Later in it's career it was providing the motive power on the Worthing Society's portable passenger carrying track, adjacent to the old L.B.&S.C.R. main line to Bognor; this event was organised by the Chalk Pits Museum at Amberley, and the B.B.C. Radio 4 team were present, taking recordings.

No. 200's exhaust beats, and also the loud and clear notes of a true Brighton whistle, were recorded for posterity.

As the last remaining "Gladstone" had been broken up 47 years previously, it is extremely doubtful if any recordings were taken of one in action. The little

The 5″ replica of "Remembrance".

Rear view lining of cab roof not quite complete. On the Sussex Miniature Loco. Society's track at Beech Hurst, Haywards Heath 13-10-74.

March 12 1980. The Post Office issue a new stamp featuring the Liverpool and Manchester Railway 1830. Brighton G.P.O. requests the loan of a vintage locomotive preferably of Brighton origin. "Gladstone" No. 200 meets the requirements and spent the day in the main Post Office in Ship Street. At the end of the day Brighton's Head Postmaster, Mr. Selwyn Veater, presents the author with a set of the new stamps.

"00" gauge electric model of "Bessborough" in umber livery built by Jim Bremner for the author.

replica therefore, was able to "speak for itself" in a manner denied to it's big sister.

The recording was broadcast in the "Breakaway" programme three weeks later and came over loud and clear.

Just after World War II, Brighton Works turned out many "Light Pacifics" of the "West Country", and "Battle of Britain" classes. Although no favourites of mine (they consumed about five times as much coal as a "Gladstone" did, from Brighton to Portsmouth and back, on the same work), they had boilers containing Nicholson Thermic Syphons.

These syphons consisted of tubes with large flat sides, rather like a fishtail, and fitted inside the firebox; to assist in the circulation of water from the foundation ring area to the firebox crown. Now whatever criticism could be directed at these "Pacifics", no one could deny it, they could certainly steam! The syphons of course, greatly assisted this. Soon after my "Gladstone" was completed, a serial appeared in the "Model Engineer" dealing with the construction of a 3½" gauge American 4-8-4 type loco., based on a very large Baldwin design for the Western Maryland Railroad.

I have always enjoyed boilermaking, and as this new design incorporated a thermic syphon, I decided that I must make one. I laid out my own arrangement of tubes and flues, before the boiler design was published, using three super-heater flues instead of the published four. Consequently, the syphon could not be fitted, as the central element of the radiant type superheater occupied the space required by the syphon.

All was not lost however, as designer Martin Evans suggested that I fit TWO syphons, one each side of the element, thus reproducing the conditions in the full size firebox. This was duly accomplished, and the boiler completed, hydraulically tested to twice working pressure, and issued with its test certificate. After fitting out, and attaching the smokebox and poppet valve throttle therein, the boiler was taken out to the Worthing Club's track at Field Place, for Steam Trials.

The enormous grate for 3½" gauge of 46 square inches, required different firing technique from the narrow grates of my other loco's, and the pressure gauge stuck obstinately on 20 p.s.i. for some time. A strong wind blowing along the unlagged, large surfaces of the all copper boiler was not helping either, but with the advent of a more even fire over the grate, pressure was eventually raised to 80 lbs, and the safety valves prevented a higher pressure than 86 lbs per sq. in. from materialising, in spite of the boiler being now worked flat out.

The test was continued for two hours, safety valves blowing continuously, and some three gallons of water was evaporated in that time.

I was well pleased with the results of this steam trial, and photographs taken of this trial look very impressive, and portray the enormous size of the later day

American boilers compared to their British counterparts.

The steam locomotive reached its ultimate size in North America just before it was superseded by Diesel traction, the largest examples producing in the region of 8,000 indicated horsepower.

The wheel has now turned full circle in my own locomotive building. The latest project is an L.B.&S.C.R. H2 "Atlantic", No. 424. This will preserve the memory of being the last full size tender loco. of the 4-4-2 wheel arrangement to run in this country.

An effort to preserve it for posterity was started, but before sufficient funds were subscribed, the powers that be cut it up. This greatly distressed me at the time, as it would have become the only full size TRUE Brighton Express loco. to be preserved, and of course would have been emblazoned with the lovely Marsh "umber" livery, with the Company's coat of arms on the splashers.

Although the preservation societies have saved some examples from the breaker's torch, which were built or worked at Brighton, to my mind they are not in the same category as the genuine L.B.&S.C.R. product. Not that I deplore the societies' efforts; I say more power to their elbow!

As my own 3½" gauge model passed out of my possession some years ago, this one will replace it; the only difference is that this time it is only half the size of my old 442, viz:– gauge "1".

With advancing years, I find the lifting of these large and heavy steam models is more than I want to indulge in now. I had more than my fair share of heavy lifting in my Erecting shop days with "Mad Jack".

The latter, incidentally, attended our club shows and admired all my Brighton loco's, right up till the end. He passed away in the summer of 1979.

The construction of my 424 is proceeding concurrently with the Baldwin 4-8-4's boiler. As the latter is now almost complete, (it is doubtful if I will build a chassis for it owing to weight restrictions mentioned above); future progress therefore, should be a little swifter than during the initial stages.

The boiler (most important appliance!) has already passed it's fitness test and steam trials. This time the chimney, dome, and safety valve cover have all been fashioned from the solid to the dimensions of the works drawings. The rest will also be so dealt with to make a really authentic copy. The livery will also be Marsh "umber", NOT Southern Green, or British Rail's "dirt colour", sorry, lined black!

It seems inconceivable to the present generation of railway enthusiasts that in "Brighton" days, the "Top link" loco's certainly, were not only spotlessly clean, they positively GLEAMED! Drivers even came in on Sunday mornings to repaint their cab roof white in their own time!

Looking back to my apprenticeship days, none of us could have perceived that our beloved loco's and even the very works itself would have passed into oblivion in our lifetime. I have done my very best to keep alive the wonderful tradition, and spirit of camaraderie that the old Brighton works deservedly enjoyed. I hope you, my readers, consider my efforts worth while; now that most of the fine old craftsmen who created these lovely L.B.&S.C.R. loco's, have passed into oblivion along with their products. May their memory remain evergreen! Au Revoir – A. C. P.

Rear view of "Remembrance" the fifth model of the author.

TAILPIECE

Towards the end of steam in Brighton Central Station. King Arthur Class No. 793 "Sir Ontzlake" collecting Pullman cars prior to departing for Victoria.

Class "E5" 0-6-2 Tank No. 570 in original condition at the main line platform of Brighton Central in 1903. These locos. were used on suburban services, and even semi-fasts to London.

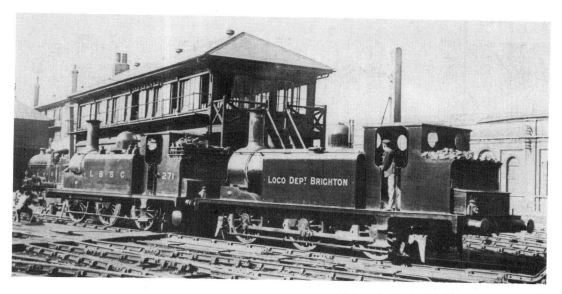

(Above) Class "E1" 0-6-0 tank loco.
No. 99 transferred to the Loco. Dept.
Moving Stroudley 0-4-2 Tank No. 271
at Brighton shed in 1919.

(Left) Cab layout of a Stroudley "Gladstone"; in Brighton Works South yard,
outside the general offices in 1922.

Immaculate freight locomotive. R.J. Billinton class "C2" 0-6-0 No. 530 in Olive Green Goods livery at Brighton Shed 1905. The class suffered from being under-boilered.

D.E. Marsh's Class "C3" freight loco. after having been fitted with L.B. Billintons "Top Feed" to the second dome in the early 1920's. This class suffered from a poorly designed chassis.

The marriage of the "C3" boiler to the "C2" chassis produced a first class freight loco. known as the "C2X" No. 447 is on the New England Road turntable. Note the buffer stops protecting the wall!

The Brighton's heavy freight class, the most powerful locos. on the line. L.B. Billinton's "K" class 2-6-0 "Mogul" introduced in 1913. They were just in time to handle the greatly increased traffic to Newhaven brought about by World War I. No. 340 is at rest on Battersea Shed.

Top link driver Fred Christmas (left) in the cab of his beloved "L" class "Baltic" tank No. 330, at Brighton Station in the early 1920's. Fireman Ray Moore on right.

A fine action shot of the down "Southern Belle" as Fred Christmas brings it within sight of Haywards Heath Station at almost 80 m.p.h. in the early 1920's. The slightly blurred appearance of the front of the loco. is due to its speed.

Class "H1" "Atlantic" No. 41 in charge of the "Southern Belle" circa 1910. These locos were very similar to the G.N.R. large boilered "Atlantics".

From October 1919 until June 1922, Stroudley "Terrier" tank engine No. 642 was shed pilot at Battersea and lettered Loco. Dept.: Note the Hull and Barnsley wagon at the rear, a rare visitor to the L.B.&S.C.R.

APPENDIX: L.B.&S.C.R. Locomotive Classes featured in this book

Class	Number built	Between dates	Number rebuilt	Withdrawn between	Built by	Numbers at 1923 and early S.R.	Boiler pressure late L.B.S.C. days	Tractive Effort at 85% boiler press	Type
A1	50	1872–1880		1901–1946	Brighton Works	635–683	150 lb/sq.in.	7,650 lb.	0-6-0 T
A1X		1911–1922	15	1925–1963	Brighton Works	635–680	150 lb/sq.in.	7,650 lb.	0-6-0 T
B1	36	1882–1891		1910–1933	Brighton Works	172–220 618, 19, 20	170 lb/sq.in.	16,043 lb.	0-4-2
B2	24	1895–1897		1907–1916	Brighton Works	171–324	160 lb/sq.in.	–	4-4-0
B2X	24+1B3	1907–1916	25	1929–1933	Brighton Works	201–213 214–324, 171	180 lb/sq.in.	15,028 lb.	4-4-0
B4	33	1899–1902		1934–1951	Brighton Works 8 Sharp Stewart Glasgow 25	42—74	180 lb/sq.in.	17,729 lb.	4-4-0
B4X		1922–1924	12	1951	Brighton Works	Between 43–73	180 lb/sq.in.	19,644 lb.	4-4-0
C1	12	1882–1887		1907–1924	Brighton Works	421–432 433–452	150 lb/sq.in.	18,402 lb.	0-6-0
C2	55	1893–1902		1935–1950	Vulcan Foundry	521–555	170 lb/sq.in.	19,094 lb.	0-6-0
C2X		1908–1940	45	1957–1962	Brighton Works	as above	170 lb/sq.in.	20,288 lb.	0-6-0
C3	10	1906		1936–1951	Brighton Works	300–309	170 lb/sq.in.	20,288 lb.	0-6-0
D1	125	1873–1887	1,toD1X	1903–1951	90 Brighton Works 35 Neilson & Co. Glasgow	221–297 354–362 633, 34, 98, 99	170 lb/sq.in.	15,186 lb.	0-4-2 T
D3	36	1892–1896		1933–1955	Brighton Works	363–398	170 lb/sq.in.	18,443 lb.	0-4-4 T
D3X		1909	2	1937–1948	Brighton Works	396–397	170 lb/sq.in.	18,443 lb.	0-4-4 T
E1	78	1874–1891		1908–1961	Brighton Works	92–164 606–611 685–697	170 lb/sq.in.	18,560 lb.	0-6-0 T
E1X		1911	1	1930	Brighton Works	689	170 lb/sq.in.	18,560 lb.	0-6-0 T

Class	No.	Built	Withdrawn	Builder	Numbers	Boiler pressure	Tractive effort	Wheel arrangement
E2	10	1913–1916	1961–1963	Brighton Works	100–109 165–170	170 lb/sq.in.	21,307 lb.	0-6-0 T
E3	16	1894–1895	1949–1959	Brighton Works	453–462	170 lb/sq.in.	22,542 lb.	0-6-2 T
E4	75	1897–1903	1944–1963	Brighton Works	463–520 556–582	170 lb/sq.in.	20,288 lb.	0-6-2 T
E4X	4	1909–1911	1955–1959	Brighton Works	466–477 478–489	170 lb/sq.in.	20,288 lb.	0-6-2 T
E5	30	1902–1904	1936–1956	Brighton Works	399–406 567–594	170 lb/sq.in.	17,359 lb.	0-6-2 T
E5X	4	1911	1954–1956	Brighton Works	401:570 576:586	175 lb/sq.in.	18,443 lb.	0-6-2 T
E6	12	1904–1905	1957–1962	Brighton Works	407–418	170 lb/sq.in.	21,216 lb.	0-6-2 T
E6X	2	1911	1957–1959	Brighton Works	407:411	175 lb/sq.in.	22,542 lb.	0-6-2 T
H1	5	1905–1906	1944–1951	Kitson & Co. Leeds	37–41	200 lb/sq.in.	19,028 lb.	4-4-2
H2	6	1911–1912	1949–1958	Brighton Works	421–426	170 lb/sq.in.	20,841 lb.	4-4-2
I1	20	1906–1907	1925–1932	Brighton Works	1–10 595–604	170 lb/sq.in.	17,433 lb.	4-4-2 T
I1X	20	1925–1932	1944–1951	Brighton Works	as above	180 lb/sq.in.	18,395 lb.	4-4-2 T
I2	10	1907–1908	1933–1939	Brighton Works	11–20	170 lb/sq.in.	17,433 lb.	4-4-2 T
I3	27	1908–1913	1944–1952	Brighton Works	21–30: 75–91	180 lb/sq.in.	19,615 lb.	4-4-2 T
I4	5	1908–1909	1937–1940	Brighton Works	31–35	170 lb/sq.in.	21,430 lb.	4-4-2 T
J	2	1910–1912	1951	Brighton Works	325–326	170 lb/sq.in.	20,841 lb.	4-6-2 T
K	17	1913–1921	1962	Brighton Works	337–343	170 lb/sq.in.	25,105 lb.	2-6-0
L	7	1914–1922	1934–1935	Brighton Works	327–333	170 lb/sq.in.	24,176 lb.	4-6-4 T
N15X	7		1935–1936	Eastleigh Works	2327–2333	180 lb/sq.in.	23,375 lb.	4-6-0
Z	8	1928–1929	1962	Brighton Works	A950–A957	180 lb/sq.in.	29,376 lb.	0-8-0 T
Sentinel Rail Car	1	May 1933	May 1935	Sentinel Wagon Works Shrewsbury	—	325 lb/sq.in.	100 H.P.	—

Locomotive Index

Photograph Acknowledgements M. Joly, A. McLeod.
Line drawings courtesy of Stephenson Locomotive Society.

General Index

Index of Persons

Allsop, Ted 69.70
Andrews, Ginger 21
Appleton, John 107.111
Austen-Walton, Jack 101

Bates, Mr. 71.73.94
Beale, Harry 73
Bennet, Peter 57
Bert. "Loo" attendant 25
Biles, Arthur 37.38
"Bill" Fitter 46.51.55.57.59.60.99
Billinton, Lawson 45.61.96.111
Brown, Mr. 26
Burfield, Jack 25
Burgess, Charlie 69

Christmas, Fred 122
Collins, "Bat" 77
Coney, Wallie 112
Coop, Bill
Cooper, Reg 28.83.84

Denny, Bill 74.93.94

Ellis, George 81.82.84.87.88
Ellis, Joe, 1st Works Manager 71
Evans, Martin 115

Felton, Harry 29
Field, Horace 74
Ford (fitter) 74
Fry, Tom 73.77.78
Fuller, Jack 101
Funnell, Harry 3.97

Gardener, G.H., 2nd Works Manager 34
Glendinning, Mr. 70
Green, Charlie 73.74.75.76.77.78

Hackett, O., 3rd Works Manager 70.77
Harmon, Dick 112
Harrington, Tom 26
Harris, K.N. 7.106.110
Hastings, Dan 81.82.83.84.87.88.91
Hebblethwaite, A.V. 105
Hefferan, Tom 25
Holl, Eric 59
Howes, Harry 95

"James", Fitter's Mate 46.59
Joly, Maurice 9.111
Jones, "Gunner" 95.96

King, Bill 81.82
Knowles, Roger 34

Long, George 74.77

"Mad Jack" 37.38.39.40.43.45.49.50.51.58.59.116
Mason, Jack 44.45.46
Maunsell, R.E.L. 34
Medical Officer 29.38
Mepham, Fred 84
Moore, Ray 124
Munro, Ernie 76

Osborne, George (fireman) 71

Parrott, Henry 34.63.65
Peake, Arthur 37.44.45.46.49.50.51.52.55.56.57.58.60.63.65.74.99
Pierce, Les 30.33
Pilbeam, Mr. 69
Pratt, Jimmy 70

Queen, Freddie 63.64.65

Ramsey, Bill 33.34.59.60
Ridge, Tom 74.75.77

Sandifer, George 73.74.75.76.77.78
Shunter, Alf 56
Slaughter, George 76.77
Smith, Ted 29.30.33.34.35.76
Stroudley, William 111.112

Thursby, George 95
Trussler, Bill 74.75

Veater, Selwyn 114

Ward, Harold 26.29.30
Watts, Bert 70
Williams, Bill 70
Woodhead, Lionel, H.B. 110.111.112
Worsley, "Ebby" 35.37.58.75.77.82.83.87.95.96
Wright, Charlie 69

Youlden, Bob 111